D1259156

The Problem of Evil

STUDIES IN ETHICS AND THE
PHILOSOPHY OF RELIGION

General Editor: D. Z. PHILLIPS

The Problem of Evil

by

M. B. AHERN

London
ROUTLEDGE & KEGAN PAUL

First published 1971
by Routledge & Kegan Paul Ltd.
Broadway House,
68–74 Carter Lane,
London, EC4V 5EL
Printed in Great Britain by
The Camelot Press Ltd.,
London and Southampton
© *M. B. Ahern 1971*
ISBN 0 7100 6998 7

Contents

Contents

Preface

This study tries to look afresh at an ancient area in the philosophy of religion. The area has great practical bearing, for it concerns the most ultimate question of all, i.e. whether God exists. Evil has persistently raised doubts about His existence. In fact, many philosophers have claimed that, given evil, there are conclusive grounds for denying that He exists. If the claim is justified, theism and, in particular, Christianity, must be based on a fallacy. Consequently, as far as truth is concerned, they should disappear and, indeed, should never have arisen. Every belief and practice that supposes them should disappear also. These are consequences which would affect profoundly the way many people live.

The study will examine this classical objection to theism but, in doing so, it will claim that the objection has been widely misunderstood and confused with other important objections, also based on evil. They must be stated and examined separately. It is one of these that most theists deal with explicitly in treating of God and evil. They consider actual evil and try to show how it can be accounted for. This is obviously an important issue. The study will ask whether such attempts give a satisfactory explanation of actual evil.

In general, it will be argued that the main arguments of both theist and non-theist fail and that evil leaves God's existence an open question.

Thanks are due to a number of philosophers for their interest and assistance. I am indebted above all to Professor

vii

viii *Preface*

H. J. McCloskey who supervised the research. With
typical patience and generosity, he set aside time, over many
months, for lengthy, weekly discussions. He read critically
many drafts. Without his encouragement and suggestions,
the study would not be published at all.

In addition, I must thank Edward Gryst, S.J., and Mr R.
Kearney for their help in the early stages of preparation
and Dr V. Rice, Mr C. A. J. Coady, Dr J. Srzednicki,
Dr G. Marshall (all of the University of Melbourne),
Mr H. Stainsby (of Monash University), J. Begley, S.J.,
C. Goodwin, S.S.S., Mr D. O'Brien, and the Editor of
this series, Mr D. Z. Phillips, for their valuable criticisms
at later stages.

I must also thank Miss L. Gorman for her skilled typing
at all stages, and the Rev. J. Opie for reading the proofs.

Introduction

Is (God) willing to prevent evil, but not able? then is he impotent. Is he able, but not willing? then is he malevolent. Is he both able and willing? whence then is evil? (*Dialogues Concerning Natural Religion*, Pt. X.)

This statement by Hume of the traditional problem of evil is typical of the way philosophers have set down the issues raised for theism by evil.[1] One of the main purposes of this study is to show that there are in fact several kinds of problem about God and evil, not one only.[2] They differ radically. Unless they are examined separately, the whole question of God and evil must be confused. Of course, if it can be shown that none is fatal to theism, it will not follow that God exists. It will follow only that no argument from the world's evil disproves His existence with logical necessity.

The terms of the problems will be taken as omnipotence, perfect goodness and evil. It is true that the problems would arise even if God's power were finite, provided that everything, except Himself, depended for its existence upon His creative power, freely exercised.[3] The complete absence of evil would then be possible and its existence would require explanation. But a being of limited power would not be the God of most believers. It would not be a fitting object of the kind of worship they give, which supposes that a greater being is inconceivable and that complete submission to God's will is justified since He cannot make mistakes. For these reasons, omnipotence will be considered one of the terms.

There are ways in which theists can avoid the problems of evil. They can be avoided by giving certain accounts of God's power or goodness. They are also avoided by giving certain accounts of evil. In each case, however, there is a price for theists to pay.

First, the problems are avoided if God is said to lack the power to prevent evil. This would entail that the world was not freely created by Him and that He is unable to intervene when evil will otherwise occur. The problems can be avoided if God is said to lack perfect goodness.[4] A god of limited goodness might be unwilling to prevent evil. But, in either case, belief in the orthodox Jewish or Christian God must be abandoned. This price must be paid. Furthermore, typical religious attitudes, such as unrestricted love, unquestioning obedience and worship of any kind would be excluded as unjustified.

Secondly, the problems do not arise for theists who hold either that evil is real but not objective in a strong sense, or that evil is not real at all. Evil may be understood by such theists solely in terms of whatever a human being[5] or a society dislikes or disapproves of; or utterances about it may be explained as merely expressing attitudes of dislike or disapproval;[6] or it may be taken to mean simply whatever God disapproves of.[7] The first two views make evil a matter of human attitude and no more; the third makes it an expression of human attitude and no more. Those who hold these views give parallel accounts of good. Since attitudes or expressions of attitudes cannot contradict one another,[8] people can differ, without formal contradiction, about what is good, about what is evil and about whether God is good or evil. Consequently, statements that God is good and something else is evil are not necessarily incompatible. This conclusion also follows if evil is defined as whatever God disapproves of. There is no logical inconsistency in a being failing to prevent what does not accord with his personal preferences.[9] Finally, any problem of evil seems to disappear if the reality of evil is denied. This may be done either by claiming that what the word refers to is illusory or by claiming that although the word refers to something real, its evilness is illusory.[10]

Theists who say that utterances about good and evil are merely utterances about attitudes or the expressions of attitudes must also hold that goodness is not an intrinsic attribute of God. They avoid every problem of evil[11] but at the cost of rejecting the usual Christian and Judaistic concept of God. Nor can they justify the common theistic belief that typical religious behaviour such as unrestricted love and unquestioning obedience are deserved and obligatory, apart from attitude. As for those who say that evil is illusory, there seems to be no sound argument to support their view. On the contrary, it seems implausible to say either that evils like pain are illusions or that, although they are real, their evilness is illusory. Furthermore, the view entails a rejection of major Judaistic and Christian doctrines, such as the Messiah and the Redemption, which suppose that evil is real.

If, then, the traditional notions of God's power and goodness are modified sufficiently, or if certain accounts of evil are given, no problem of evil arises. But other problems crucial for religious belief do arise.

Does evil necessarily raise problems for any theistic position which maintains that God is unlimited in power and goodness and that evil is real and objective, apart from attitude? Theists claim either that the existence of God can be rationally established independently of evil, or that their religious beliefs are wholly or partly non-rational. These positions will be briefly considered and it will be asked whether any of them avoids the problems.

Those who assert that the existence of God can be rationally established apart from evil claim that the fundamental question about the world is not the origin of evil but the origin of things, in themselves not evil, without which there would be no evil, so that logically the origin of evil is a secondary question. They claim that the only rational account of how it is that something exists rather than nothing is that an uncreated being produced the world. They claim that analysis of what such a being must be like shows that it is necessarily omnipotent and wholly good.

According to this view, the existence of God can be established rationally, so long as there is a world, and whether or not it contains evil. Many philosophers deny this, but if it can be substantiated it will follow necessarily that there are answers to the problems of evil even if they are not yet known. On the other hand, if it can be shown that the existence of God is logically incompatible with evil, the view cannot be substantiated, for evil does exist. Philosophers have claimed that this can be shown. Hence, the theists in question should disprove the claim either by showing that it has not been established or by showing positively that God and evil are not logically incompatible.

Theists who describe their theism as partly non-rational believe that, although reason cannot give certainty about God's existence, it can establish it as probable or even as highly probable.[12] They point to a number of facts which, they say, are best explained if there is a God, e.g. religious experience. The value of reasons like this one does not concern us here. What concerns us is that there are theists whose theoretical position is the one described. Certainty about God's existence comes from faith but it is not entirely non-rational, for it is thought to be supported by reason. If, however, God and evil are logically incompatible, the existence of God is no longer even probable on rational grounds and faith in Him is certainly irrational. Evil therefore raises problems for these theists too.

Finally, those who say that their religious beliefs are wholly non-rational contend that faith alone gives grounds for accepting God's existence. But if evil is logically incompatible with God's existence, their faith must be misplaced. A claim that God and evil are incompatible calls for refutation by them also.[13]

It seems, then, that evil raises problems for every theistic position which holds that God is omnipotent and wholly good, and that evil is real and objective, independently of human attitude.

NOTES

[1] The term 'evil' will be discussed later. It refers to certain actions like murder, and to certain states like blindness or pain.

[2] All such problems will be taken as problems about logical compatibility. But it is possible to argue that *synthetic a priori* principles make God and evil incompatible. This view will be noted in the conclusion.

[3] Could the world depend wholly on God and yet be eternal and uncreated? Aquinas' final position was that this cannot be shown to be impossible (*Summa Theologiae*, Pt. 1, Q.46, A.2). If it is possible, the problems would still arise since God would have the power to prevent evil actually occurring. This question will not be discussed further.

[4] But, in view of the amount of actual evil, *all* of the problems could be avoided only by placing extreme limits on God's goodness; *some* could be avoided if God were merely good or very good, and not wholly good.

[5] Cf. John Hick, *Evil and the God of Love*, London, Macmillan, 1966, pp. 12–15.

[6] E.g. C. L. Stevenson, *Ethics and Language*, New Haven and London, Yale University Press, 1944, Chs. 1 and 2; A. J. Ayer, *Language, Truth and Logic*, London, Victor Gollancz, 1964, Ch. 6.

[7] E.g. Ockham, 4 Sent. 9, E-F.

[8] Contradiction is usually taken to refer to statements, not to attitudes. Attitudes may conflict, e.g. one person may wish to destroy what another wishes to preserve. The attitudes of two people about the same thing may diverge and not conflict, e.g. in cases of liking and aversion; and there can be degrees of divergence. It is impossible for the one person to have simultaneously certain divergent attitudes about the same thing, e.g. great loathing for and great interest in cricket unless, perhaps, one attitude is unconscious. But it is possible for one person to have divergent attitudes about different things.

[9] In so acting, a being need not be irrational. It could take into account the preferences of other beings.

[10] E.g. Mary Baker Eddy, *Science and Health with Key to the Scriptures*, Authorized Edition, 1934.

[11] An attempt to reconcile, logically, approval of God with disapproval of evil in creation is justified if good and evil are understood, at least in part, as intrinsic to things, not if they are explained solely in terms of attitude. The attempt will succeed only if God's intrinsic goodness can be reconciled with the world's intrinsic evil. Of course, even if they are reconciled, psychological and spiritual problems may remain.

[12] A belief that God certainly exists even though the rational support for the belief is only a probability argument may be considered partly non-rational and partly rational.

[13] Particular theists of this kind may refuse to examine the problems, e.g. because, convinced by faith of God's reality, they believe the claim cannot be established. There seems nothing irrational in this approach, but it leaves the claim unrefuted.

1

'The Problem of Evil' and the Problems of Evil

There are many problems concerning evil, some of them practical and others speculative. How to prevent a specific evil is a practical problem of evil. Since such problems are not philosophical, they will not be discussed at all. Historically, one speculative problem about evil has been considered so important that it has been called 'the problem of evil'. This is the problem whether the existence of an omnipotent and wholly good God is compatible with the existence of *any* evil.

It will be argued that the whole subject of God and evil has been in a confused state, due to failure to separate questions that are different and to keep in clear view the precise nature of each question. It will be shown that, centrally, there are three distinct kinds of problem about the logical compatibility of God and evil. It will be maintained that the traditional problem of evil is fundamentally an abstract problem and that it is a problem about evil in general. It will be claimed that besides the traditional problem (soon to be called the general problem of evil), there are other, distinct problems (to be called the specific problems of evil) which concern specific evil. Some of these are fundamentally abstract problems which ask whether the existence of God is compatible with specific evil. The others are concrete problems which ask whether the conditions for compatibility are met in our world. The former class of

I

problem will be called the specific abstract problems of evil and the latter class will be called the specific concrete problems of evil. There will then be three kinds of problem about the logical compatibility of God and evil designated:

(1) The general problem;
(2) The specific abstract problems;
(3) The specific concrete problems.

It will be argued that it is essential to distinguish the general problem of evil from the specific problems and that it is essential to distinguish the abstract problems, whether general or specific, from the concrete problems.

This study is concerned with both the general and the specific problems.[1]

The Nature of the Traditional Problem

First, it must be shown that the traditional problem of evil is both abstract and general.

An early formulation of the problem was given by Epicurus (342/1–270 B.C.). Lactantius (c. A.D. 260–c. A.D. 340) quotes him as follows:

> God either wishes to take away evils, and is unable; or He is able, and is unwilling; or He is neither willing nor able; or He is both willing and able. If He is willing and unable, He is feeble, which is not in accordance with the character of God; if He is able and unwilling He is malicious which is equally at variance with God; if He is neither willing nor able, He is both malicious and feeble and therefore not God; if He is both willing and able, which is alone suitable to God, from what source then are evils? or why does He not remove them?[2]

In Christian centuries, the same problem has often been stated and discussed, most notably by St Augustine and St Thomas Aquinas. Writers commonly attribute to Augustine the following statement of the problem:

> Either God cannot abolish evil or He will not: if He cannot then He is not all-powerful; if He will not then He is not all-good.[3]

St Thomas, apparently subsuming omnipotence under the notion of infinite goodness, states the problem thus:

> If one of two contraries is infinite, the other is excluded absolutely. But the idea of God is that of an infinite good. Therefore if God should exist, there could be no evil. But evil exists. Consequently God does not.[4]

Among the writings of non-theist philosophers on this matter those of Hume are classical. His statement of the problem is concise:

> Is (God) willing to prevent evil, but not able? then is he impotent. Is he able, but not willing? then is he malevolent. Is he both able and willing? whence then is evil?[5]

In our own day, the same puzzle has been vigorously presented again. J. L. Mackie, writing in *Mind* in 1955, expressed it in this preliminary way:

> The problem of evil . . . is a logical problem, the problem of clarifying and reconciling a number of beliefs . . . in its simplest form the problem is this: God is omnipotent; God is wholly good; and yet evil exists.[6]

H. J. McCloskey writes in a later article:

> The problem of evil is a very simple problem to state. There is evil in the world; yet the world is said to be the creation of a good, omnipotent God. How is this possible? Surely a good omnipotent God would have made a world which is free of evil of any kind.[7]

Despite certain differences in the way they formulate it, all of these writers, from Epicurus to McCloskey, raise the same basic problem, the problem whether it is possible for both a totally good, omnipotent being and *any* evil to exist. Some formulations say explicitly why this is a problem and others do not. They all agree that the problem arises as soon as its three notions are understood—namely, the notions of a wholly good being, of an omnipotent being, and of evil. Since part of the notion of a wholly good being is that it is always opposed to evil, and since the notion of an omnipotent being entails that it can bring about whatever it wills, it seems that the existence of both a wholly good, omnipotent being and any evil is excluded by the notions themselves. Consequently Mackie calls the traditional problem of evil 'a logical problem, the problem of clarifying and reconciling a number of beliefs'.

A problem of this kind does not depend on what the world is actually like.[8] Neither the stating of the problem nor the answering of it need suppose any matter of fact. It may therefore be called an abstract problem.

This point can be brought out in another way. Given the three notions concerned,[9] the problem can be expressed hypothetically—that is, independently of whether or not evil actually exists. It can be asked: If any evil should exist, could a wholly good, omnipotent being also exist? To answer this question it will not be necessary to discuss actual cases of evil and to show whether the evil is justified, with respect to God. It will be enough to show whether, if evil were to exist, some instance of it *could* be justified.

The traditional problem of evil is also a general problem. Unlike the notions of omnipotence and perfect goodness, when they are taken together, the notion of evil admits of kinds, degrees and multiplicity. The next chapter will note that evil, in its primary sense, may be said (i) of the free acts of persons, (ii) of the physical states of persons and animals, and (iii) of the psychological states of persons and animals. This divides evil into very different kinds, moral, physical and psychological. The degree in which each kind may occur can vary. As well, there can be one or more instances of each kind and degree. But, the traditional problem of evil prescinds from specific kinds, degrees and multiplicity of evil and arises simply with the notion of evil. For this reason, it will be called the general problem of evil. The writers quoted above implicitly recognize the general nature of the problem. Augustine, St Thomas, Hume, Mackie and Mc-Closkey all speak of 'evil', not of this or that kind, degree or number of instances of evil. St Thomas argues that, if God exists, there could be 'no evil' and McCloskey requires, in the full theist hypothesis, 'a world free of evil of any kind'.[10]

Although Epicurus speaks of 'evils', it is clear that his basic argument does not depend upon kinds, degrees or multiplicity.

This point is of capital importance. If the traditional problem of evil is a genuine one, it stands or falls with the notion of any evil at all, even the slightest. Arguments to show that its terms are logically incompatible must hold whenever the notion 'evil' is verified. If they fail in any case, they fail completely, for they will not have shown that it is contradictory to assert the existence of both God and evil. Consequently, it is irrelevant to the problem to stress specific gross evils as some philosophers have done. For example, McCloskey, having set down the problem in the terms cited, lists some of the more distressing examples of evil, such as 'the excruciating pain of the slowly dying child whose body has been bruised and broken by a landslide'[11] and 'a particularly cruel, brutal murder'.[12] He wants to show that 'evil is (not) something trivial that could almost be brushed aside'.[13] However, if the problem is the kind it is said to be, namely a problem about the logical compatibility of omnipotent goodness and *any* evil, it is independent of these or of any other specific examples. Problems about the co-existence of God and specific evil will be other problems about God and evil.

The introduction of examples of evil is indeed one of the causes of the confusion, already mentioned, which is to be found in many treatments of this problem of evil. Emphasis on examples draws attention away from the precise problem which is supposed to be under discussion—that is, the abstract and general problem stated above. It makes it appear that specific examples are part of that problem whereas the problem fully exists apart from them. It suggests the need for solutions to the specific problems raised by the examples as if such solutions must be part of the solution to the general problem. Furthermore, since the examples are usually taken from the actual world, it gives the impression that the general problem concerns the actual justification, not the possible justification of evil. Theists, in their turn, increase the confusion by attempting to offer solutions to specific problems in the apparent belief that they are discussing and trying to solve the traditional, abstract and general problem of evil.

The truth is that the general problem of evil is different from the specific problems presented by examples of evil and is, in fact, the fundamental problem about God and evil. It is fundamental because if its terms are logically incompatible, no examination of examples of evil is needed, for there is no longer any problem of God and evil to solve. That is to say, if it is contradictory to assert both the existence of God and *any* evil, as some philosophers have argued it is, and evil of any kind exists, the existence of God is automatically excluded. There will then be no problem of reconciling God's existence with specific examples of evil. If, however, it is not contradictory to assert both the existence of God and some evil, or if it cannot be shown to be so, problems about the existence of God and specific evil will need to be raised.

If there is to be clarity about the question of God and evil, it seems essential to distinguish the general problem of evil, the problem whether the existence of even one instance of any kind and degree of evil of itself logically excludes the existence of a God who is both wholly good and omnipotent, and the specific problems of evil—that is, whether the existence of this or that kind, degree or multiplicity of evil excludes the existence of such a God.

The present chapter and succeeding ones will use this distinction to keep separate questions which are not the same.

The Nature of the Specific Problems

The second thing to be established in this chapter is that some of the specific problems of evil are fundamentally abstract while others are concrete problems.

It could seem that the general problem is the only abstract problem about God and evil—that is, the only problem which could be asked and answered quite apart from the actual nature of the world. This is not so, however. The preceding section noted that evil can differ in kind, degree and number of instances, so that problems may be raised about specific evil as well as about *any* evil. These problems may be abstract. About each *possible* specific kind, degree and number of instances of evil it may be asked: Is the existence of God compatible with this evil? In every case, the problem is fundamentally abstract both because it does not depend on whether or not the specific evil exists[14] and could be asked if it did not exist, and because answers to it need not suppose any fact about the actual world. These problems will be called the specific abstract problems of evil.

It is clear why specific abstract problems must be raised as well as the general abstract problem. If the terms of the general problem are not logically incompatible, or if they are not shown to be so, it will follow only that at least one instance of evil is compatible with the existence of God, or that the opposite has not been shown. It will not follow that each possible evil is compatible with God's existence. It might be the case that while it is not contradictory to assert the existence of God and of one kind of evil, say physical evil, it is contradictory to assert the existence of God and of another kind of evil, say moral evil. There might be special features about moral evil which make it impossible for it to be justified. In the same way, it might be the case that although a small degree of some kind of evil is compatible with the existence of God, a greater degree of the same kind of evil is not. Thirdly, it might be the case that one or a few instances of evil could, logically, co-exist with God but that many instances could not. There are, therefore, specific problems of evil which are abstract problems.

Abstract problems are not the only ones which can be raised concerning specific evil. These problems ask whether, in the case of some specific evil, the existence of God is compatible with the evil. Affirmative or indefinite[15] answers to these problem will entail only that, if the evil exists, the existence of God is compatible with it or that the contrary cannot be proved. They will not entail that the conditions for compatibility are met in fact. Good which, if it existed, could justify the evil, may never actually exist. Because the abstract problems are fundamentally independent of all matters of fact, they can go no further. They are concerned, not with whether evil is in fact justified, but with whether, if evil exists, it *could* be justified.[16] They require no discussion of whether good to justify evil does exist.

Hence, if evil actually exists, other, distinct problems must be raised about it. About each actual evil it must be asked: Are the conditions under which this evil is compatible with the existence of God in fact met? That is: Does justifying good actually exist? This is a new series of problems about God and evil. In this study, they are called the specific concrete problems, since both the stating of them and the answering of them depend necessarily on facts about the world. Unlike the abstract problems, no concrete problem can be stated unless some actually existing evil is referred to and none can be definitively answered unless the actual state of the world is referred to.[17]

Of course, if it were already shown that the terms of one or more of the specific abstract problems were logically incompatible, and if the evil or evils in question actually exist, the concrete problems, will not arise. It will then follow that one or more instances of evil exist which are necessarily incompatible with the existence of God. It will be pointless to ask whether the conditions for compatibility are met in the case of actual evil which is compatible with God's existence, for the existence of God will already have been positively excluded. But, before the specific abstract problems are examined, it cannot be assumed that their terms are logically incompatible. Hence, the concrete problems must be regarded as legitimate and also as different from the specific abstract problems.

Part of the discussion of the abstract problems could take account of the actual world by asking whether, with respect to God, the good in it could justify the evil. If particular instances of evil could be justified by actual good, it will follow that those evils are logically compatible with the existence of God. On the other hand, if no actual good able to justify certain evils is found, it will not follow that justifying good is not possible. The abstract problems about these evils will then remain. We shall see later that, because of certain facts about the world, little light would be thrown on the specific abstract problems by taking actual good into account. For this reason, and also because the abstract problems concern any logically possible justification while the concrete problems concern actual justification, it seems better to raise the question whether actual good could justify the world's evil in dealing with the concrete problems and not in dealing with the abstract problems. The chapter on these problems will refer to the actual world, but only to its evil, not to good in it which might justify the evil.

So far, this chapter has been concerned to show that there are, centrally, three distinct kinds of problem about the logical compatibility of God and evil. These are:

(1) The general problem, i.e. is the existence of God compatible with *any* evil?

(2) The specific abstract problems, i.e. is the existence of God compatible with specific evil?

(3) The specific concrete problems, i.e. are the conditions for compatibility met in our world?

Avoiding Confusion about God and Evil

It has been argued in this chapter that the traditional problem of evil is fundamentally abstract and general, that there are distinct problems about specific evil, some abstract, some concrete, and that all the abstract problems must be distinguished from the concrete problems. Philosophical writings about God and evil have rarely taken account of these points, e.g. philosophers have often run together the general problem and the specific problems or not distinguished abstract from concrete problems. It seems possible that the origin of much of this confusion is the actual use made of the term 'the problem of evil'. The traditional problem alone has often been called 'the problem of evil'.

The same term has also been used about other problems of evil, either on their own or together with the traditional problem. In philosophy, 'the problem of . . .' often refers to a number of problems about the same matter, e.g. knowledge or universals, but it is not then also used as if the matter raises only one problem. In the case of evil, the double use of the term may easily have been a source of confusion.

The expression 'the problem of evil' can be taken in at least four ways. It can refer (i) to the general problem, or (ii) to the specific abstract problems, or (iii) to the specific concrete problems, or (iv) to any and every problem about the logical compatibility of God and evil, i.e. to both the general and the specific problems. Ambiguity would be partly avoided if the first three meanings were distinguished by a terminology like that used in this chapter. In this way it would be made clear before a discussion began what 'the problem of evil' was to mean throughout the discussion. Use of the new terminology in the discussion itself would achieve still greater clarity.

What of the fourth sense of the expression? It seems to be a fact that when people speak of 'the problem of evil' they often refer to any and every problem about the logical compatibility of God and evil. It is then important that they say this explicitly. But that is not enough. The differences which exist between the general problem and the specific problems on the one hand and, on the other hand, between the abstract problems, whether general or specific, and the concrete problems, are so great that all these problems cannot be discussed together. A terminology like the one adopted in this chapter is again needed, and since the three kinds of problem are being referred to, any discussion of 'the problem of evil' in this fourth sense must use the terminology throughout. Otherwise, the differences between the kinds of problem and between the kinds of solution they require will again be obscured.

Would it be preferable to abandon altogether the expression 'the problem of evil' because of its past ambiguous usage? This probably would be preferable. Since, however, the expression is likely to remain in use, it seems essential to accept the suggestion just made if a discussion about God and evil is not to be seriously confused.

NOTES

¹ The authors of a recent book on God and evil claim that 'if the problem of evil were stated as a formal contradiction the theist would have no difficulty whatever in rebutting it' (Edward H. Madden and Peter H. Hare, *Evil and the Concept of God*, Springfield, Illinois, Charles C. Thomas, 1968, p. 4). They refer here to the traditional or general problem and hold that it would be absurd to think that the co-existence of a wholly good, omnipotent being and of *some* evil is logically impossible. Historically, however, the problem is a celebrated one which has received close attention up till the present time. Nelson Pike notes that 'John Stuart Mill, J. E. McTaggart, Antony Flew, H. D. Aiken, J. L. Mackie, C. J. Ducasse and H. J. McCloskey are but a very few of the many others (who have believed there could be no solution to this problem)' (*God and Evil*, ed. Nelson Pike, Englewood Cliffs, New Jersey, Prentice-Hall Inc., 1964, pp. 86–7). Indeed Mackie believes that this problem leads to a positive disproof of God's existence ('Evil and Omnipotence', *Mind*, Vol. LXIV, No. 254 (1955)) and McCloskey claims that 'evil is a problem for the theist in that a contradiction is involved in the fact of evil on the one hand and the belief in the omnipotence and perfection of God on the other; God cannot be all-powerful and perfectly good if evil is real' ('God and Evil', *Philosophical Quarterly*, Vol. X, No. 39 (1960)). Hence, the general problem of evil is still an actual and important problem which deserves careful examination. A second reason for examining it is that if its terms can be shown to be logically incompatible, it will be pointless to examine any of the other problems.

² The original text reads: '. . . Si vult et non potest, imbecillis est; quod in Deum non cadit. Si potest et non vult, invidus; quod aeque alienum a Deo. Si neque vult, neque potest, et invidus et imbecillis est; ideoquo neque Deus. Si vult et potest, quod solum Deo convenit, unde ergo sunt mala? aut cur illa non tollit?' (*Patrologia Latina*, VII, 121). 'Invidus' is sometimes translated 'envious' (John Hick, *op. cit.* p. 5, n. 1; except for the word 'envious', the translation he quotes has been used above) but 'malicious' seems to fit the context better.

³ But they do not give the reference, e.g. John W. Steen, 'The Problem of Evil: Ethical Considerations': *Canadian Journal of Theology*, Vol. XI, No. 4 (1965). The substance of the quotation can be found in *Confessions*, Bk. 7, Ch. 5.

⁴ *Op. cit.*, I, Q.2, A.3.

⁵ David Hume, *Dialogues Concerning Natural Religion*, Pt. X.

⁶ *Op. cit.*

7 'The Problem of Evil', *Journal of Bible and Religion*, XXX, 3 (1962).

8 It may, however, be occasioned by the actual nature of the world. This was in fact the case with the traditional problem of evil, as the formulations quoted show. It was suggested by actual evil. But, fundamentally, the problem is abstract, as Mackie points out. It makes God's existence doubtful only indirectly, i.e. in so far as we know beforehand a fact which lies outside the substance of the problem—namely, that evil exists.

9 Whether we would, in fact, have the notion 'evil' if we never experienced evil does not affect the present point.

10 It is true that these writers discuss other problems of evil. But, in doing so, they fail to notice that the problems go beyond the original problem stated.

11 'The Problem of Evil', *Journal of Bible and Religion*, XXX, 3 (1962).

12 *Ibid.*

13 *Ibid.*

14 It does not of course exclude the actual existence of the evil. In either case, the abstract problem is identical.

15 I.e. that the terms of the problems cannot be shown to be logically incompatible.

16 In a recent book, D. Z. Phillips rejects all justification theories about the world's evil and God (*The Concept of Prayer*, London, Routledge & Kegan Paul, 1965; New York, Schocken Books, 1966; Ch. 5). This kind of view will not be examined explicitly.

17 The views that evil is justified because it is necessary for the best possible world and that a world without evil is impossible will be rejected elsewhere.

2

Terms

Each of the kinds of problem of evil distinguished in the first chapter was taken to have the three terms, omnipotence, perfect goodness and evil. Evil may be either *any* evil, or specific evil. These terms will now be discussed. It will be shown how they are related to the problems of evil.

Omnipotence

At least four accounts of divine power can be given:

(1) God can bring about whatever it is logically possible for a being of unlimited power to bring about;

(2) God can also bring about what is logically impossible;

(3) God's power is limited, but everything, except Himself, was freely created by Him;

(4) God's power is limited and He neither created the world nor can prevent the evil which occurs in it.

As the Introduction noted, theists who hold the fourth view avoid every problem of evil, but they must face other problems. Those who hold the third view do not avoid the problems but they meet the further problem that their God seems to be neither the God of most believers nor an appropriate object of the worship most believers give. Hence these accounts of divine power will now be disregarded.[1] Does either of the other two correctly define omnipotence?

Aristotle gives the following definitions of the possible and the impossible:

The impossible is that of which the contrary is of necessity true, e.g. that the diagonal of a square is commensurate with the side is impossible, because such a statement is a falsity of which the contrary is not only true but also necessary.

The possible is found when it is not necessary that the contrary is false, e.g. that a man should be seated is possible; for that he is not seated is not of necessity false.[2]

These definitions concern the logically possible and impossible. The logically possible is that whose concept does not contain contradictory elements, and the logically impossible is that whose concept does contain contradictory elements. If the elements of a concept are not contradictory it follows that the concept can be instantiated; it does not follow that the concept is instantiated. If the elements of a concept are contradictory, the concept can never be instantiated. It is a pseudo-concept which refers to nothing at all.

Omnipotence is unlimited power to bring things about. The only things a being of unlimited power can bring about are those which it is logically possible for the being to bring about. Hence, omnipotence is the power to bring about whatever it is logically possible for a being of unlimited power to bring about. Consequently, whatever it is logically impossible for *any* agent to bring about is excluded, e.g. that a past event did not occur. Secondly, things which, though logically possible for certain agents, suppose limited power are excluded, e.g. to produce something its maker cannot control. Philosophers sometimes use this example when questioning whether omnipotence is a coherent notion. They speak of the paradoxes of omnipotence. Thus, J. L. Mackie, in discussing whether an omnipotent being can make things which it cannot subsequently control, argues that neither an affirmative answer nor a negative answer seems satisfactory. An affirmative answer will mean that once such things have been made, the being will no longer be omnipotent. A negative answer will mean that there is something an omnipotent being cannot do.[3] Mayo gave the following reply to the paradox: 'Since "things which an omnipotent being cannot control" is a self-contradictory phrase, to make such things is logically impossible . . . failure to bring about logical impossibilities does not count against omnipotence.'[4] This reply was cautiously accepted by Mackie.[5] It seems likely that other paradoxes of omnipotence can be answered in a similar way.

Some philosophers have argued that the account given above is an account, not of omnipotence, but of limited power. It puts upon power the limit that it cannot extend to what is logically impossible. For example, Descartes says:

> Pour la difficulté de concevoir, comment il a été libre et indifférent à Dieu de faire qu'il ne fût pas vrai, que les trois angles d'un triangle fussent égaux a deux droits, ou généralement que les contradictoires ne peuvent être ensemble, on (dit) que la puissance de Dieu ne peut avoir aucunes bornes.[6]

and

> Pour les vérités éternelles, je dis . . . que sunt tantum verae aut possibiles, quia Deus illas veras aut possibiles cognoscit, non autem contra veras a Deo cognosci quasi independenter ab illo sint verae.[7]

But since the logically impossible or the contradictory is nothing at all, not to be able to bring it about is no genuine limitation on power. Similarly, inability to bring about things, in themselves logically possible, which entail a lack of power, does not tell against omnipotence. As Aquinas says in his classical discussion, it is more accurate to say that whatever is logically impossible cannot be done than that omnipotence cannot do it.[8] Hence, the only correct account of omnipotence is that it is the power to bring about whatever it is logically possible for a being of unlimited power to bring about.

Another objection sometimes made is that since God is wise and good as well as powerful, there are things which He cannot bring about, even though they are neither logically impossible nor entail a lack of power, e.g. to create a world of ice-cream and nothing else. The answer is that if God cannot do such things it is not because He has no power to do them, but because, being wise and good, He will not use the power He has. In a similar way, there are many things a good man has the power to do which he will not do because he is good.[9]

It seems that a being unlimited in power must also be unlimited in knowledge, at least with regard to everything it can bring about. Certain possible states of affairs suppose knowledge, e.g. that an event which would otherwise occur is prevented by intervention. An omnipotent being must be able to bring things about in all of the ways it is logically possible for them to be brought about by a being with unlimited power, in every possible order, at any time and with no possibility of mistake. This seems to require an exhaustive knowledge of things, of their powers and their possible relationships with and effects upon other things. Accordingly, it seems that an omnipotent being must be omniscient, at least with respect to everything logically possible apart from itself. It is not clear that it must be omniscient about itself as well. Omniscience of this kind might be called relative omniscience.

There need, of course, be no problem of evil if it were logically impossible for evil not to exist. But it is not logically impossible. It is conceivable that a world without evil should exist, or that there should be no world at all. It is also conceivable that a world should exist with some evils and not with others. Hence, an omnipotent being could prevent all evil or certain specific evils. But omnipotence is not sufficient for the problems of evil to arise. It is not contradictory to assert that an omnipotent being exists and that evil exists. An omnipotent being, as such, is neither opposed nor disposed to evil. The problems of evil can arise only if God is also wholly good.

Perfect Goodness

Theists commonly claim that God is wholly good and that goodness is an intrinsic attribute of His nature. The kind of goodness in question is moral goodness. Moral goodness is the goodness of a free intelligent agent. But, moral goodness is not identical with moral perfection. We attribute it to people who are morally imperfect. Most people fail morally, e.g. they are sometimes dishonest, unkind, selfish. But unless they fall well below a certain standard of moral goodness we call them morally good. Nevertheless, we recognize degrees of moral goodness. We say that some people are morally better than others.

A morally perfect being acts well always. It is morally good in so far as it acts well and morally perfect in so far as it acts well always and never evilly. Failure to act in an evil way is not itself a sufficient condition of perfect moral goodness: a permanently insane person is neither good nor evil morally. But a single evil act is a sufficient condition of the lack of perfect moral goodness. It would be contradictory to assert that the same being was both perfect and, in some respect, evil morally. Consequently, if a being is morally perfect it will never be true that moral evil can be predicated of the being.

The Introduction noted that the problems of evil are avoided, at a price, when certain accounts of goodness are given. There need be no problem of evil if perfect goodness is not a divine attribute. A being which was not wholly good might lack the goodness to prevent evil. But, besides being perfectly good, God must be powerful enough to prevent evil for any problem of evil to arise. Hence, the problems of evil are unavoidable only if God is both wholly good and sufficiently powerful. However, discussion of these problems must centre on goodness. As the previous section showed, there can be no doubt that an omnipotent God could prevent all evil. Theist and non-theist can agree on that. The fundamental dispute between them is this: Is it logically necessary to predicate evil of God, who is said to be wholly good and omnipotent, if any evil or if specific evils exist? Alternatively: Is it logically possible for a being to be wholly good if it causes evil, or if it could prevent evil but does not do so? The non-theist must show that it is not logically possible. The theist must show either that it is logically possible, or that it cannot be shown to be logically impossible. If he can do the first, the theist will have shown that the existence of God and evil, either in general or specific evil, are not logically incompatible. If he does the second only, the theist will have shown that logical incompatibility cannot be established.

Evil

There are three kinds of evil: moral, physical and psychological evil.[10] In its primary sense, moral evil is the evil of a free intelligent agent which chooses what is known to be morally wrong.[11] What is chosen can vary greatly: it may be something unjust, dishonest, selfish and so on. In its secondary sense, moral evil refers to what is chosen, apart from whether an agent knows that it is immoral to choose it, e.g. taking another's property without justification. When we call such things morally evil we mean that no one, aware of their nature, can deliberately choose them without moral evil in the primary sense. Physical evil includes such evils as bodily deformities, lack of limbs and bodily powers, sickness. Psychological evil is pain and suffering. Physical and psychological evil seem able to occur in both human beings and in animals. Many degrees and multiple instances of each kind of evil are possible. Moral evil varies in degree according to what is done, e.g. murder is a greater evil than stealing, and according to the motive and to the malice with which it is done. Malice increases as awareness of the evil increases or as the deliberation with which it is done increases. Physical and psychological evil can vary in degree too. It is a greater physical evil to lose the sight of both eyes than to lose the sight of one. Some pains are worse than others. There can be an indefinite number of instances of each degree of the three kinds of evil. As the previous chapter showed, any instance of evil at all raises the traditional or general problem of evil. Specific instances, which can vary in the ways just described, raise specific problems.

'Evil' is often used in a secondary sense. For example, houses where black magic is practised have sometimes been called evil houses. The houses are not evil in themselves.

They are called evil, in a transferred sense, because they are associated with evil activities. We are not concerned with such secondary senses. Causes of evil such as earthquakes, hurricanes, germs and poisonous insects, are often called evils. But they are not evil in themselves and so do not create a new kind of evil. The problem: Is the existence of God compatible with this physical evil caused by a hurricane? is identical with the problem: Can God be justified in causing or in not preventing this physical evil?

The Introduction indicated some of the objections to be met by those who deny that evil is real or that it is objective in a strong sense. Since these views avoid every problem of evil, this study concerns only those philosophers who assert both the reality of evil and its objectivity, apart from attitude. Is evil, then, necessarily something positive? H. J. McCloskey has argued that the Thomist privation theory of the nature of evil makes evil not fully real.[12] This theory states that evil consists in the lack, not of possible good, but of proper or due good. Thus, the lack of red corpuscles in a man, but not in a fish, is a real evil with real effects. If it were not real, it could have no effects. McCloskey himself seems inclined to admit that certain evils (the loss or lack of organs) are privations of proper good. Yet these evils are fully real. The important question, then, is not whether any evil is privative in nature but whether all evils are. The theory is intended to cover all evils. But it is doubtful whether a privative account of pain is possible. Few Thomists examine this matter in detail and those consulted who do are not convincing.[13] Scholastic philosophers have thought that unless a privative account of every evil could be given, evil must be predicated of God as the actual Creator of those evils which have a positive nature. However, in the next chapter it will be argued that, under certain conditions, God could cause non-moral evil without blame. If this is so, there is no *a priori* reason for holding that all evil must be privative. As for moral evil, it is arguable that a privative account of it can be given.[14] It seems, then, that some evils are positive in nature and others, while fully real, are privative.[15]

CPE

NOTES

[1] John Stuart Mill (1806–73) argues, e.g. that since an omnipotent God would always achieve ends without means and since there are countless examples in this world of the achieving of ends by means, God's power, if He exists, must be finite (*Theism*, ed. Richard Taylor, New York, the Liberal Arts Press, 1957). The answer to this objection is clear. Provided that the means are not logically necessary, a being which cannot achieve ends without means is not omnipotent. A being which can achieve ends without means but does not do so may be omnipotent. William James (1842–1910) holds that God's nature is developing. He must struggle with evil. Both God and men can assist one another towards realizing their potentialities. James writes: 'In saying "God exists" all I imply is that my purposes are cared for by a mind so powerful as on the whole to control the drift of the universe' (R. B. Perry, *The Thought and Character of William James*, Boston, Little, & Co., 1936, Vol. I, p. 737). Alfred North Whitehead (1861–1947) also believes that God's nature is evolving and claims that evil testifies to this fact. Every actual being has both a physical and a mental pole or aspect. God is finite and in process with respect to the physical pole of His nature (*Process and Reality*, New York, Macmillan, 1929, p. 521). The problems of evil are avoided by such theories only if they deny of God free creative power.

[2] *Metaphysics*, Bk. V, Ch. 12.

[3] 'Evil and Omnipotence', *Mind*, Vol. LXIV (1955).

[4] 'Mr Keene on Omnipotence', *Mind*, Vol. LXX, No. 278 (1961).

[5] 'Omnipotence', *Sophia*, Vol. I, No. 2 (1962).

[6] *Œuvres de Descartes*, ed. C. Adam and P. Tannery, Paris, 1905, Vol. 4, p. 118.

[7] *Op. cit.*, Vol. I, p. 149.

[8] *Op. cit.*, I, Q.25, A.3.

[9] Some philosophers claim that certain theists understand omnipotence to imply that God will exercise, or is likely to exercise, power whenever He can (D. Z. Phillips, *The Concept of Prayer*, p. 100; Rush Rhees, *Without Answers*, London, Routledge & Kegan Paul, 1969; New York, Schocken Books, 1969; pp. 112–13; cf. Simone Weil, *Waiting on God*, London, Routledge & Kegan Paul, 2nd impression, 1952, pp. 86–7). Plainly, omnipotence does not imply either of these things. There is no necessary connection between power and its exercise. A theist who attributes omnipotence to God is not thereby committed to anything about its use.

[10] For present purposes, the usual way of classifying kinds of evil will be followed.

[11] Strictly, it may be claimed that moral evil exists even when what is deliberately chosen is falsely believed to be morally wrong. This complication will be disregarded here.

[12] 'The Problem of Evil', *Journal of Bible and Religion*, XXX, 3 (1962).

[13] E.g. A. D. Sertillanges, *Le Problème du Mal*, Paris, 1951, Vol. 11; Charles Journet, *The Meaning of Evil*, London, Geoffrey Chapman, 1963.

[14] See Jacques Maritain, *God and the Permission of Evil*, trans. Joseph W. Evans, Milwaukee, the Bruce Publishing Co., 1965.

[15] Even if all evil could be shown to be privative, the problems of evil would remain. (See M. B. Ahern, 'A Note on the Nature of Evil', *Sophia*, Vol. IV, No. 1 (1965); H. J. McCloskey, 'Evil and The Problem of Evil,' *Sophia*, Vol. V, No. 3 (1966); M. B. Ahern, 'The Nature of Evil', *Sophia*, Vol. V, No. 3 (1966).)

3

The General Problem

The traditional problem of evil is this: Is the existence of God compatible with *any* evil? It is an abstract problem, i.e. a problem which can be stated and answered apart from any matter of fact, and a general problem, i.e. a problem, not about specific kinds, degrees and multiplicity of evil but about any evil at all, even the slightest.

It seems clear that no claim that the terms of the problem are logically incompatible can succeed without supporting argument. There does not seem to be even a *prima facie* contradiction between the statement that an omnipotent being exists which is wholly good and the statement that another being exists which is evil in some respect. Statements which are plainly contradictory are these:

(1) An omnipotent being exists which is wholly good.
(2) The same being is evil or powerless in some respect.

To make a successful claim that the terms of the problem are logically incompatible, it will be necessary to add principles logically connecting evil in one being with evil or lack of power in God, who is said to be wholly good and omnipotent. An argument that the co-existence of God and evil is logically impossible must fail unless the apparent logical gap in the claim that evil in the world logically excludes perfect goodness and power in God is closed.

One method of examining the general problem of evil, therefore, is to enquire whether satisfactory principles can be found. A different method is to ask whether any evil could be morally justified if an omnipotent, wholly good God exists.[1] These methods, though distinct, are related. If some evil could be justified, or the opposite cannot be shown, it will not be possible to find the required principles. If, however, evil could never be justified when God is the agent, the principles can be found. The general problem will be now examined by both methods, but the latter will be used first for two reasons. It will throw light on whether or not the required principles can be found. Secondly, it is, in itself, a more conclusive method. The other method will consist in examining the most plausible principles suggested by philosophers. Taken on its own it will be decisive only if suitable principles are found. If they are not found, a critic can object that suitable principles may yet be discovered.

Examination by the First Method

If evil could be justified, good seems to be the only thing which could justify it. The good would have to arise on the occasion of evil; otherwise it would be irrelevant. It would have to be proportionate to the evil; otherwise, it would not justify the evil. Whether in fact evil could be justified by good with respect to God will be best answered by first enquiring if it is ever true, e.g. with respect to human agents, that evil can be justified by good, and if it is, under what conditions it is true.

Can evil be justified by good? This question implies that the occurrence of an evil is in the control of some personal agent. When, in daily life, we call an evil accidental we usually prescind from any control God may have over it and mean that it was not deliberately caused by any human being. We might then say that the evil was compensated for by good. We would not say that it was justified by good.[2] There is no doubt, however, that, at least as far as human agents are concerned, we accept, under certain conditions, the principle that evil can be justified by good. The principle has two senses. It can mean either that:

(1) The direct causing of evil, whether by physical or by moral means,³ can be justified by good,

or that

(2) the non-prevention of foreseen evil can be justified by good.

Under certain conditions, we accept the principle in both senses with regard to human agents.

Surgery is an obvious example of non-moral evil brought about by physical means. We believe that, normally, a surgeon is morally justified in operating despite the evil. But we assume certain things. We assume that:

(1) What is done is designed to produce good proportionate to the evil.

(2) The good cannot be achieved without the evil, in any way possible for the agent.⁴

There seem to be necessary conditions for justifying any non-moral evil caused directly by physical means. In some cases, they are also sufficient conditions, but in others, a third condition is assumed:

(3) The agent has at least the tacit consent of the person who suffers the evil.

These are many cases in which this condition does not apply. They may concern minors or the mentally ill. They may also concern responsible adults, e.g. a motorist would be justified in slightly injuring one person to avoid injuring another person seriously, even though he knew that the first person would never agree to his so acting. Again, civil authorities could override the objections of adults who refused treatment during an epidemic. It seems, then, that the only conditions which must always be met when non-moral evil is directly caused are the first two.

However, from the fact that an evil is justified, it does not follow that an agent is necessarily blameless in causing it. His intention may be evil in some respect. Thus, although a surgeon cannot avoid intending the physical evil he causes, if his action is to be fully good morally, he must intend it only as a means to good and in no way for its own sake. Otherwise, he will have an evil intention which, it may be claimed, can never be justified with respect to the agent who has it. Pain which merely accompanies surgery need not be intended at all. Unless an accompanying evil such as pain is a means to known good, it must not be intended, if an agent is to be morally blameless.

Non-moral evil can also be caused directly by moral means, e.g. by giving permission for surgery. Consent of this kind may be called positive permission. It may be given willingly or unwillingly. The manager of a business might consent willingly to his employee's seeing his doctor in working hours. A father might consent unwillingly to his daughter's marriage, if she insists on it. He would have a double wish: the wish that no marriage occur and the wish that, if his daughter insists, it occur. The latter wish is a state of positive permission.

Positive permission, given willingly or unwillingly, has direct influence on the doing of an action. It may be said to cause the action directly but morally. Since non-moral evil caused directly by physical means may be justified, positively permitting it may also be justified. It will be justified if the conditions set out above are verified.[5]

So far, only non-moral evil has been considered. Can the direct causing of moral evil be justified by good? Opinions on this differ. Some say that the direct causing of moral evil can never be justified, e.g. it is always wrong to defraud in order to give a donation to charity.[6] Some say that the direct causing of moral evil can always be justified by good, others that the question does not arise since what is morally evil always depends on circumstances. The first view is the least favourable to this study and it will be assumed by it. However, certain complications arise when God is the agent. These will be noted later.

Understood in its first sense, then, the principle 'evil can be justified by good' is generally accepted, under certain conditions, at least with regard to non-moral evil. That is to say, in the case of human agents, we commonly accept the principle that the direct causing of non-moral evil, either physically or morally, may be justified by good. It will be justified if the required conditions are met.

The second sense of the principle is this: the non-prevention of foreseen evil can be justified by good. Cases in which someone fails to prevent an evil which he foresees are very common.[7] A swimming instructor may foresee that a person about to receive his first lesson will accidentally swallow sea-water and, as a result, suffer nausea. He may also foresee that this person will experience muscular pain and fatigue because he will train hard. Yet, he may decide that he is justified in not preventing these evils by the greater good of his pupil's learning to swim. In some sense, the instructor causes the evils for although he foresees them he helps to create the circumstances in which they will occur. He could have prevented them by refusing to instruct or by refusing the use of his swimming pool. This sense of causing evil is very different from the sense in which an instructor would cause it if he either physically forced his pupil to swallow sea-water and to train hard or persuaded him to do so. It may be called causing evil indirectly.

When a person causes something indirectly, he deliberately creates conditions which he foresees will lead to it. He may be said to permit it negatively or passively. He may not intend the occurrence itself either as a means or as an end. He may have no will about it except the negative one of not preventing it. It is possible that he even wants it not to happen and perhaps warns against it. Nevertheless, in creating the circumstances in which it will happen, he fails to prevent it and this requires moral justification if the thing concerned is evil.

Often we do not question that failure of this kind by human agents is justified. We do, however, then assume that certain conditions are fulfilled. When the evil is non-moral the following necessary conditions must be met:

(1) What is done is designed to produce good proportionate to the evil.

(2) The good cannot be achieved without the evil, in any way possible for the agent.

As with the first sense of the original principle, a third condition is sometimes required, namely:

(3) The agent has at least the tacit consent of the person who suffers the evil.

As before, there are many cases in which this condition does not apply, e.g. in the case of minors and even in the case of responsible adults. Thus, a city council might be justified in fluoridating the water supply without the consent of the citizens although it foresaw that some would suffer side-effects. Accordingly, the first two are the only conditions which must always be met if failure to prevent non-moral evil is to be justified.

It was noted that when evil is caused indirectly, it need not be intended in any way. But the examples used indicate an important difference between possible cases. Foreseen evil may not itself contribute to good in any way known to an agent, or it may be the known occasion of some good. A swimming instructor may know of no good which can come about through nausea itself, but he may believe that muscular pain and fatigue will help his pupil to swim better by stimulating him to greater will-power. Indeed, it may be the case that most people become good swimmers only if they have gone through training which results in physical suffering.[8] He would then be morally justified in intending the muscular pain and fatigue in view of the good they occasion but he would not be justified in intending the nausea at all. It follows, at least in instances of non-moral evil, that whether a person who creates circumstances in which evil will arise, and so fails to prevent the evil, can be justified in intending the evil will depend on whether the evil is itself the occasion of proportionate good. A similar distinction was made about instances of non-moral evil directly caused.

So far, only examples of non-moral evil have been used about the second sense of the principle that evil can be justified by good. What is to be said if the evil is moral? Can good justify the non-prevention of foreseen moral evil? We commonly accept that it can. For example, moral evil would be prevented if people did not have any children. It can be foreseen that if children are born they will at some time commit moral evil. Yet, if there were no children, great good would be lacking. We do not hold people morally blameworthy because they do not radically prevent moral evil by refusing to have children at all.

Again, parents sometimes allow their children to do things, e.g. join one of the Forces, or go overseas alone, although they believe that new moral challenges will not always be met successfully by them. Absolutely speaking, they could prevent this moral failure, but they may believe that failure, as well as other circumstances, may itself be the occasion of moral growth which could not otherwise occur. We believe that such parents are often morally justified.

These cases show that we accept the principle that the non-prevention by human agents of foreseen moral evil may be justified by good. They also show that the conditions under which it is commonly thought that the non-prevention of moral evil can be justified by good when human agents are in question are the same conditions as those under which the non-prevention of non-moral evil can be justified. Often the third condition will not be applicable.

Of course, those who believe that it is never right to cause moral evil directly will also maintain that, in not preventing moral evil, it is never right to intend the evil even as a means to good.

The foregoing discussion of the principle 'evil can be justified by good' can be summarized by making comparisons between the two senses of the principle, between what can and cannot be justified by each sense, and between the conditions under which evil can be justified.

First: The two senses of the principle. Causing evil directly is very different from causing evil indirectly. Whoever causes evil directly does something which produces the evil.[9] The agent must intend the evil itself either as a means or as an end, except when evil merely accompanies an action. Whoever brings about evil indirectly does something which occasions the evil. The agent need not intend the evil itself in any way.

Secondly: What can and cannot be justified. It may be claimed that none of the following can be justified:

(1) Causing evil, either directly or indirectly, disproportionate to the good sought.[10]

(2) Directly causing moral evil.

(3) Causing evil, either directly or indirectly, when the good sought could be achieved by the agent without the evil.[11]

It may be claimed that under certain conditions, either of these can be justified by good:

(1) Directly causing non-moral evil.

(2) Not preventing foreseen moral or non-moral evil.

Thirdly: The conditions under which evil can be justified. These are:

(1) What is done is designed to produce good proportionate to the evil.

(2) The good cannot be achieved without the evil, in any way possible for the agent.

In some cases a third condition is required:

(3) The agent has at least the tacit consent of the person who suffers the evil.

However, an agent who meets these conditions will not be morally blameless if his intention is evil in some respect. Thus, it may be claimed that he must not in any way intend for its own sake the non-moral evil he directly causes; he must not intend accompanying evil at all unless it is a means to good; he must not intend non-moral evil which he fails to prevent unless it is a means to good and he must not intend moral evil even as a means to good.

Although all examples used so far concerned evil brought about by human agents, the conclusions drawn were general ones. They seem to apply no matter who the agent may be.[12] If this is so,[13] some instances in which evil is brought about could never be justified, and other instances would be justified, even if the agent were God, provided that the conditions were met. Could the conditions ever be met if God were the agent? It is the second condition which raises a doubt. It says that for evil to be justified by good, the good must be unable to be achieved without the evil, in any way possible for the agent. In medicine, if a patient's health can be more easily restored without surgery, a surgeon is not justified in operating. A physician is not justified in using treatment which causes greater evil than equally effective treatment which causes less. If God were the agent, however, everything would be possible except what is logically impossible for a being of unlimited power. The second condition, applied to God, can therefore be expressed more clearly in this way: the good could not be achieved without the evil in any way that is logically possible for a being of unlimited power. It is not obvious that there can be such good.

The first condition, namely, that what is done is designed to produce proportionate good, modifies the second by stipulating that the good it refers to must be proportionate to the evil.[14] Hence if God were the agent, it could not be disregarded. Both conditions can be expressed together thus: proportionate good could not be achieved without the evil, in any way that is logically possible for a being of unlimited power.

As for the third condition, it seems clear that if it would ever apply in God's case, it could be met, as far as He is concerned. But it may be argued that the condition would never apply, partly because, before creation, the question of consent would be excluded since there would be no one to give consent, and partly either because God's relationship to human beings would always be analogous to that between parents and children or because His status as Creator would be privileged. It seems, then, that in God's case the third condition would never apply as a necessary condition. For the general problem it is enough that there could be some instance in which it would not apply and in which the other conditions could be met.

What has been said about the subjective intention of human agents if they are to be morally blameless would apply if God were the agent. But if He is wholly good, His intention would always be good and never evil.

The kinds of cases of causing evil which might be able to be justified if God were the agent, together with the conditions for their justification, can now be stated:

Concerning moral evil: God might, without blame, fail to prevent moral evil, which He in no way intended, if it would be the occasion of proportionate good which, logically, could arise in no other way.

Concerning non-moral evil: God might, without blame, directly cause non-moral evil for the sake of proportionate good if, logically, the good could arise in no other way. He might, without blame, fail to prevent it, and even intend it, if it were logically necessary for the achieving of proportionate good.

These statements set out what instances of evil might be justified, given the existence of a wholly good, omnipotent God, and the conditions under which they would be justified. They contain, therefore, the necessary and sufficient conditions under which the general problem of evil can be solved and, indeed, under which any abstract problem of evil can be solved.

Could these conditions ever be met?

The conditions in each statement are that there should be good which, logically, supposes the existence of some evil and that the good should be proportionate to the evil. It does not seem possible to show that these conditions could never be met. The notion 'good' does not itself entail that whatever instantiates it could not logically suppose either moral or non-moral evil, or that the good could not be proportionate to the evil. If this is true, there seems to be no way of showing that the conditions could never be met. There will then be no way of showing that the terms of the general problem of evil are logically incompatible, i.e. of showing that, if any evil exists, moral evil must be predicated of God.

Secondly, in fact, there seem to be goods which, logically, could arise only on the occasion of evil. Mercy and forgiveness seem to be examples of these goods. Some virtues, such as fortitude, could be fully developed, it seems, only through an element of trial by evil of some kind. Personal faith and trust in God could grow in certain ways only through the testing of faith and trust in God's total goodness and power occasioned by evil. Benevolence towards others suffering evil supposes evil. Any single, genuine example will be enough to show that this condition could be met. It appears that the condition could be met.

It seems, too, that the other condition, namely, that good which logically supposes evil should be proportionate to the evil, could be met. For example, it may be claimed that moral and spiritual good, such as that illustrated above or the good of friendship mentioned by Wisdom,[15] could be more valuable than freedom from the evil concerned and that some notable degree of it could be occasioned by a minor degree of evil. It seems then that the second condition, if the existence of a wholly good, omnipotent being is to be compatible with evil, could be met. For the general problem of evil, a single, satisfactory example will suffice. It seems possible for such an example to be found.

For these reasons, it seems that the general problem of evil can be solved, that is, it seems logically possible for some evil to be justified by good, even if God exists.

This method of examining the general problem has led to two conclusions, one of them negative and the other positive. They are:

(1) It is impossible to show that the existence of *any* evil is logically incompatible with the existence of God.

(2) It seems possible to show that the existence of *some* evil is logically compatible with the existence of God.

Examination by the Second Method

We take up now the alternative method of examining this problem. It rests on the fact that there seems to be no direct contradiction in asserting that an omnipotent being which is wholly good exists and that another being exists which is evil in some respect. For an argument from the fact of evil to the non-existence of God to be logically cogent, it must employ principles which show a logically necessary connection between evil in the world and lack of power or goodness in God. If the preceding examination of the general problem is sound, it will not be possible to find them.

Commonly, philosophers try to supply the required principles, at least by implication, but they rarely attempt to show by analysing and discussing them either that they are satisfactory or that they are not satisfactory.[16] For example, Hume implicitly uses the principle: A being which is able but not willing to prevent evil is malevolent; but he assumes that it is self-justifying. Augustine implicitly uses the principle: A being which will not abolish evil when it can is not all-good; but he does not explicitly show why it is (as he believes) unsatisfactory. Yet, such principles are crucial. If they are satisfactory, the existence of God will have been certainly disproved, given the fact of evil. If they are unsatisfactory, His existence will remain an open question. The most plausible principles suggested by philosophers will now be examined in order to see whether or not they can close the logical gap in the traditional argument from evil to the non-existence of God. It will be argued that they are all in fact false and that, if restated and made analytically true, they still fail.

One test any suggested principle must meet is that it is analytically true. The reason is that it must establish, with logical necessity, a link between evil in the world and imperfect power or goodness in God, should He exist. Otherwise, the existence of evil will not be logically incompatible with the existence of omnipotent goodness.[17] Only analytically true principles can forge this link. Principles which are merely synthetically true are insufficient: they will never entail imperfection in God. What, then, are the chief principles suggested by philosophers? Are they analytically true?

Principles about power can be dealt with quickly. It is easy to supply analytically true principles about power and many philosophers have done so, e.g.:

Epicurus:	A being which is willing to take away evils and is unable, is feeble.[18]
Hume:	A being willing to prevent evil but not able is impotent.[19]
J. L. Mackie:	There are no limits to what an omnipotent being can do.[20]

In view of the contention of the previous chapter[21] that it is logically possible for there to be no evil, the general problem cannot be solved by claiming that although God is omnipotent, He cannot prevent evil. It follows, too, that the key principle to be supplied by anyone who asserts that both God and evil could not logically co-exist, must concern goodness. Principles about goodness used by Epicurus, Augustine, Hume, Mackie and R. D. Bradley will now be studied. First it will be asked whether they are analytically true. If they are not, it will then be asked whether they are satisfactory when reformulated as analytically true principles.

Epicurus, Augustine and Hume use principles sufficiently similar to be taken together:

Epicurus:	A being which is able to take away evil and unwilling to do so is malicious.[22]
Augustine:	A being which will not abolish evil when it can is not all good.[23]
Hume:	A being which is able but not willing to prevent evil is malevolent.[24]

Since the general problem of evil concerns not merely the removing of existing evil but the preventing of every evil, Hume's principle is to be preferred to the other two.

It does not seem possible to make out even a *prima facie* case that Hume's principle is analytically true. No doubt a being may be malevolent because it is unwilling to prevent the evil it can prevent, but it is not necessarily malevolent on that account. A major part of this chapter was spent in showing that there are several kinds of case in which a being which does not will to prevent the evil it can prevent is nevertheless a morally good being. The non-prevention of both moral and non-moral evil may be morally justified. It will be justified if certain conditions are met.[25] In fact, the direct causing of non-moral evil may be justified and, under certain conditions, will be justified.[26]

Consequently, Hume's principle is not analytically true. It is therefore incapable of making a logically necessary connection between evil and the non-existence of God. Indeed, since Hume must intend it as a universal principle, the principle is not true at all.

No objection to this argument can be based on the fact that while human agents are limited in power, God is omnipotent. Hume's principle concerns power as such, whether limited or unlimited. It makes a general claim about any agent, human or divine, who can prevent some evil. If a particular agent cannot prevent an evil, it is untouched by the principle. But, any agent which can prevent it is covered by the principle.

As it stands, therefore, Hume's principle entails that no agent can be morally justified in not preventing evil which it can prevent. This suggests that it says more than Hume intended: it is unlikely that Hume would want to deny that human agents can sometimes be justified in not preventing evil. The principle can be restated so that it takes account of cases in which an agent is justified in failing to prevent evil. It will then read:

A being which is able but not willing to prevent evil is malevolent, unless it is justified in not preventing the evil.

This principle seems to be both true and analytically true. But, it is no more successful than Hume's in establishing an analytic connection between the fact of evil and the non-existence of God. It is true, but irrelevant, that the conditions under which evil can be justified by good apply differently in the case of human agents and in the case of God. In God's case, the good must be unable to be achieved in any other logically possible way. But, if the first part of this chapter is accepted, good seems possible which, logically, supposes evil, and is proportionate to the evil or, at least, it cannot be shown that it is not possible. Consequently, even when Hume's principle is restated and made analytically true, it does not entail the non-existence of God if any evil exists. It fails to meet a second test of any suggested principle, namely, that it does connect logically *any* evil in the world with the non-existence of God.

Mackie offers an explicit principle about goodness. This is:

Good is opposed to evil in such a way that a good thing always eliminates evil as far as it can.[27]

Like Epicurus and Augustine's principle, Mackie's is not expressed accurately enough. One can eliminate only what already exists. If evil exists before the principle begins to apply, the use of the principle will be vitiated, for that evil will be untouched by it. However, this defect can be remedied by substituting 'prevents' for 'eliminates'. The principle will then read: 'Good is opposed to evil in such a way that a good thing always prevents evil as far as it can.'

It is evident that this principle is neither true nor analytically true; all of the points raised against Hume's principle apply to Mackie's. It often happens that the non-prevention of evil is justified, or that the direct bringing about of evil is justified. Accordingly, the principle is simply false. It could be restated and made analytically true, as Hume's principle was. But, then it would be equally incapable of logically connecting any evil and the non-existence of God, for either the non-prevention of evil seems able to be justified in God's case, or the contrary cannot be shown. Hence, Mackie's principle, in either version, cannot show that if evil exists, God cannot.

R. D. Bradley has recently proposed a principle which amounts to this:

A being which is responsible for evil through not prevent-ing it when it could is not wholly good.[28]

This principle, like Mackie's, is false. There are cases in which someone may be indirectly responsible for either moral or non-moral evil (because he does not prevent it) and yet be morally blameless. He may be morally justified in not preventing the evil. There are cases in which someone may be directly responsible for non-moral evil (because he pro-duces it) without being morally blameworthy. Consequently, this principle is neither true nor analytically true. Like the other suggested principles, it can be made analytically true, but it would still be incapable of linking with logical necessity the existence of any evil with the non-existence of God.

At one place in his article, Bradley states his principle in another way. It may be taken as a separate principle worth examination. It is this:

If a being is willing that evil exists, then it is not perfectly good.[29]

The phrase 'is willing' is ambiguous. It can be used when someone wants an evil to occur for its own sake, or when he wants it to occur for the sake of good. The evil may be either moral or non-moral. It can be used when someone does not want an evil to occur but passively permits it to occur (by not preventing it) for the sake of proportionate good. Certain of these instances can be justified and others cannot. It may be claimed that it is never justifiable to want or to directly bring about moral evil either as a means or as an end, and that it is never justifiable to want or to directly bring about non-moral evil for its own sake. But, it may be justifiable to want and to directly bring about non-moral evil for the sake of propor-tionate good and it may be justifiable not to prevent either kind of evil for the same reason and therefore to will it in some indirect sense. Accordingly, this principle, like all of the others, is false. Like the others, too, it can be made analytically true but with no better result. It will be unable to connect logically the fact of evil with God's non-existence.

Several of the most plausible principles explicitly or implicitly proposed by philosophers to connect, with logical necessity, the terms of the general problem of evil have now been examined. All of them fail for the same reason. Each is simply false and therefore none is able to meet the first thing required of a satisfactory principle, i.e. that it is analytically true. Any of them can be made analytically true but then none of them will meet the second requirement, i.e. that it links logically any instance of evil with the non-existence of God.

No doubt other similar principles could be suggested. It seems likely, however, that they would all fail in the same ways. Furthermore, if the argument of the first section of the chapter is sound, it is not possible to find satisfactory principles.[30]

When both studies are taken together, it may be claimed:

(1) It cannot be shown that, if *any* evil exists, a wholly good, omnipotent being could not exist.

(2) It seems possible to show that a wholly, good, omnipotent being could exist, if *some* evil exists.

In either case, it will follow that philosophers[31] who have claimed that the existence of evil entails a positive disproof of God's existence are mistaken. It will also follow that the traditional problem of evil seems able to be solved or, at least, that it is not possible to show that it cannot be solved.

NOTES

[1] This is equivalent to the question whether an omnipotent, wholly good God could be justified in either directly causing or not preventing evil. It will be seen shortly that 'justification' supposes an agent. Here the agent concerned is God.

[2] 'Compensation' concerns the counter-balancing of an evil by good. Often it supposes blame on someone's part. A person may be morally blameworthy for having directly brought about the evil or for not having prevented it. He may be merely legally blameworthy. In either case, his conferring some good

on the person who suffered the evil, or on a related person, such as a wife, may be called compensation. The good compensates, fully or partly, for the evil. At other times, however, blame on someone's part is not supposed. For example, we might say that good health compensates a patient for evil caused by surgery. There are secondary uses of the term also, e.g. it can be used when some good accompanies some accidental evil. Hence 'compensation', in its primary sense, may be used, in a purely human context, whether or not an evil is justified. In every case, a good which compensates is contrasted with an evil which is compensated for. In every case, too, the good is conferred on the person who suffered evil, or on a related person.

'Justification' of evil by good differs from the primary sense of 'compensation' in several respects. The person compensated is the person injured, but the person justified is the person who in some way brings about the evil. Compensation directly concerns the counterbalancing of evil by good but justification directly concerns the moral standing of a person who brings about evil. Compensation is possible only when a person suffers evil, but justification is possible when evil is suffered either by a person or by an animal. Finally, compensation for evil does not suppose that the evil was justified, but justification of evil seems to suppose that the evil is compensated for.

3 'Moral means' is here contrasted with physical means, not with immoral means. Thus, we speak of 'moral pressure'.

4 This condition supposes that there are no other relevant considerations, e.g. experiment, or convenience and expense in relation to a particular evil. If there are, the conditions will apply with respect to both goods taken together.

5 What was said about 'intention' concerning non-moral evil caused by physical means also applies when the evil is caused by moral means.

6 But it does not follow that not preventing the evil cannot be justified. Furthermore, those who hold the view might justify persuading someone bent on doing evil to do the lesser of two evils. This could be construed as decreasing evil rather than as causing it. Such cases will not be considered further.

7 In many of these cases, e.g. when someone fails to prevent a quarrel between people whom he does not know, the person who does not act may have done nothing which could lead, even indirectly, to the evil. Such cases do not concern this study.

8 There are, in fact, many good things, such as the mastery of difficult studies, sport or certain skills, which cannot usually be achieved by us without, for example, anxiety and strenuous effort.

9 Justification of evil, but not compensation for evil, entails that the evil is brought about deliberately.

10 E.g. carrying out a very painful medical procedure which will add only a few minutes to a patient's life.

11 Unless there are other relevant considerations (cf. n. 4 above).

12 Theists commonly say that God could give human beings leave to do things which it would otherwise be wrong for them to do, e.g. to give to

charity property belonging to another. But in the view already accepted, namely, that the direct causing of moral evil is wrong, God could not be justified in directly causing someone to give another's property to charity unless he also gave leave for this to be done. Moreover, there are certain things which God could neither give permission for nor directly cause without moral blame, e.g. to hate what is good.

William of Ockham (*c.* 1280/90–1349) took the opposite view, arguing that God could always directly cause what we call moral evil, or approve it, while remaining wholly good. He said:

By the very fact that God wills something it is right for it to be done . . . Hence, if God were to cause hatred of Himself in anyone's will, that is, if He were to be the total cause of the act (He is, as it is, its partial cause) neither would that man sin nor would God; for God is not under obligation, while the man is not (in the case) obliged, because the act would not be in his power. (*Loc. cit.*, quoted in Frederick Copleston, S.J., *A History of Philosophy*, New York, Image Books, Doubleday, 1963, Vol. 3, Pt. 1, p. 116.)

The part of Ockham's claim which is of special interest here is that what is good or evil depends on the divine free-will so that, in every case, God could will what was formerly morally evil without ceasing to be perfectly good. As the Introduction noted, this view avoids the problems of evil but at a heavy price. However, rejection of it raises the question whether morality is independent of God and, if it is, how God could be the Absolute. But, if what is moral does not depend solely on the divine will, it does not follow that it is independent of God. It may be claimed that it depends on the divine nature, known by God's mind, which every created thing reflects in some way. Accordingly, it may be claimed that what is good is founded, not on some independent source, but on the divine nature which God wills necessarily. However, this raises issues too large to be treated here.

¹³ Aquinas holds that since God, by one and the same act, wills everything that He wills, his willing ends cannot be the *cause* of His willing means. He adds that, nevertheless, God wills means on account of ends (*op. cit.*, 1, Q.19, A.5). Accordingly, the first condition is not substantially affected by his view.

¹⁴ Thus, a minor good would not justify great evil. 'Proportionate' is best explained by pointing to commonly accepted illustrations, like those used in this chapter. They show that in cases of evil, some caused directly and others indirectly, we recognize that there are goods proportionate to evil. Accordingly, we know what the first condition means. But, when evil is directly caused, is good proportionate to the evil always possible? Those who say that the direct causing of moral evil can never be justified, with respect to the agent who causes it, will deny that it is always possible. As far as other kinds of evil are concerned, we do not seem able to show that proportionate good is not always possible, for we have no adequate knowledge of possible good. For the same reason, it seems impossible to show, in cases of evil indirectly caused (i.e.

not prevented), that there could not always be good proportionate to the evil. Of course, in particular cases we may believe that there is in fact no such good, with respect to human agents.

15 Although John Wisdom does not explicitly distinguish the general problem of evil from other problems, he argues that there are cases of evil justified by good, e.g. 'Some of the best sorts of friendship depend on the fact that in them are fully manifested all kinds of affection . . . triumphant affection must contain not only the rejoicing affection of the present but the power of transcending affection and the memory of sorrow and lament . . . false memories would not serve as well as genuine memories' ('God and Evil', *Mind*, Vol. XLIV, No. 173 (1935), pp. 18, 19).

16 But it will be seen shortly that there is no need for analysis or discussion in the case of principles about power.

17 As the Introduction noted, this thesis is concerned only with logical compatibility. But it will be claimed that the principles about goodness soon to be examined are false as well as non-analytic. Hence, they could not succeed even as suggested *synthetic a priori* principles.

18 This principle is implicit in Epicurus' statement, 'If (God) is willing and unable (to take away evils) he is feeble' (Ch. 1, p. 2).

19 Implied by Hume's formulation 'Is God willing to prevent evil, but not able? then is He impotent' (Ch. 1, p. 3). This principle is preferable to Epicurus' since the general problem of evil concerns the total prevention of evil, not merely the taking away of pre-existing evil.

20 'Evil and Impotence'. Mackie's principle, taken in the sense that omnipotence extends to whatever it is logically possible for a being of unlimited power to bring about (which is not a genuine limit) has already been accepted. (Ch. 2).

21 Ch. 2, p. 16.

22 This principle underlies Epicurus' statement: 'If (God) is able (to take away evils) and unwilling He is malicious' (Ch. 1, p. 2).

23 The words attributed to Augustine are: 'If (God) will not (abolish evil) then He is not all-good' (Ch. 1, p. 2).

24 Hume's actual words are: 'Is (God) able (to prevent evil), but not willing? then is he malevolent' (Ch. 1, p. 3).

25 See p. 31.

26 See p. 31.

27 *Op. cit.*, H. J. McCloskey implicitly accepts this (*Philosophical Quarterly*, Vol. X, No. 39 (1960)).

28 'A Proof of Atheism', *Sophia*, Vol. VI. No. 1 (1967).

29 *Ibid.*

30 The following principles are sometimes suggested:

(1) A being which does not prevent unnecessary evil when it can is malevolent.

(2) A being which does not prevent avoidable evil when it can is malevolent. However, unless 'unnecessary evil' and 'avoidable evil' mean evil which is

unjustified, the principles will not be analytic. But if this is what the terms mean, the principles will not succeed, for reasons already given.

[31] See Nelson Pike's claim quoted earlier that 'John Stuart Mill, J. E. McTaggart, Antony Flew, H. D. Aiken, J. L. Mackie, C. J. Ducasse and H. J. McCloskey are but a very few of the many others (who have believed there could be no solution to this problem)' (*op. cit.*).

4

The Specific Abstract Problems

The specific problems of evil are related to the traditional problem in two ways.[1] First, they are related negatively, for if it could be shown that it is contradictory to assert the existence of God and any evil at all, the specific problems would be excluded absolutely. But if the claim of the last chapter that this cannot be shown is accepted, the specific problems can arise. Secondly, they are related positively, for if, as the chapter attempted to show, some evil could be justified if God exists, or the contrary cannot be proved, it is not obvious why it would be logically impossible for other evil to be justified. Apart from these links with the traditional problem, the specific problems are independent.

Every instance of evil, whether it is actual or merely possible, raises the abstract problem: Is the existence of God compatible with this evil? In each case, the problem is abstract both because while not excluding the actual existence of the evil, it does not suppose it, and because answers to the problem do not necessarily suppose any matter of fact about the world.[2] These are the specific abstract problems. Only those about actual evil are important. No objection to God's existence can be based on evil which is merely possible and never becomes actual. It is only actual evil which can call in question the existence of a wholly good, omnipotent being. Accordingly, this chapter will examine the question: Is the existence of God compatible with actual evil, i.e. is it logically possible for actual evil to be justified with respect to God?

Many writers do not recognize the specific abstract problems as a distinct kind of problem. Madden and Hare are exceptional: they distinguish between the abstract and concrete problems.[3] But they make no study of the former. These are important for the following reasons. First, if it could be shown that it is logically impossible for some specific actual evil to be justified with respect to God, His existence would be disproved and the concrete problems would be ruled out. All theories intended to show that actual evil is in fact justified would then be pointless. Objections to them would be equally pointless. Both the theories and the objections suppose it has not been shown that it is logically impossible for actual evil to be justified. Secondly, since the last chapter claimed that the non-existence of God cannot be established, with logical necessity, through the general problem, and the final chapter will make the same claim with respect to the concrete problems,[4] the only other possible way of establishing His non-existence is through the specific abstract problems. Unless it can be done through them, evil will never provide logically adequate grounds for rejecting the existence of God.

Actual evil comprises all past, present and future evil. It is vast in variety and in amount. For these and other reasons given later,[5] it is not possible to specify all instances of actual evil. But it is generally considered that there are three kinds of it, that there are many degrees of each kind and that there are probably many instances of each degree. Thus, there is moral evil, e.g. injustice; hatred; greed; violence; there is physical evil, e.g. injury; illness; loss of bodily parts, such as an arm or a leg; loss of bodily powers, such as hearing: there is psychological evil, e.g. pain and suffering.[6] Many degrees of each kind of evil exist, e.g. murder is a greater moral evil than lying, the loss of a hand is a greater physical evil than the loss of a finger, and severe pain is a greater psychological evil than slight pain. Finally, there are probably many instances of each degree of evil. Accordingly, the abstract problems about specific actual evil can be examined in a general way by asking these questions:

(1) Is the existence of God compatible with each kind of actual evil?

(2) Is the existence of God compatible with every degree and multiplicity of actual evil?

Only one claim about the specific abstract problems will be made, namely that it seems impossible to show that the existence of God is incompatible with actual evil.

About Kinds of Evil

First, is the existence of God compatible with each kind of evil?

This question leaves aside the degree or multiplicity in which evil actually occurs. If a kind of evil is logically incompatible with the existence of God, the degree or number of instances in which it occurs will be irrelevant. The slightest degree and a single instance of the kind will be incompatible. Hence the question really means: Is the existence of God compatible with any degree at all of moral or non-moral evil, even in a single instance?

In fact, this question was discussed in the previous chapter on the general problem. In itself, the general problem concerns any evil at all and prescinds from particular kinds of evil. But there can be no instance of evil which is not evil of a particular kind. Consequently, in answering the general problem by the first method, the chapter stated the necessary and sufficient conditions, in God's case, for justifying moral evil and conditions for justifying non-moral evil.[7] It then gave two arguments about kinds of evil, one indirect and the other direct.[8] The direct argument tried to show by example that both sets of conditions could be met. Since, however, it is not possible to give a direct argument about degrees and multiple instances of evil, no use will be made here of the argument with respect to kinds. The indirect argument was as follows:

The notion 'good' does not itself entail that whatever instantiates it could not logically suppose either moral or

non-moral evil, or that the good could not be proportionate to the evil. Therefore, it seems impossible to show
positively that God could not be morally justified in not
preventing some instance of either moral or non-moral
evil.

This argument was supported when the general problem
was examined by the second method. The principles studied
were all stated in terms of evil in general. But, examination
showed that they were false in the case of both moral and
non-moral evil and if changed into analytically true principles it seemed impossible to show that the condition they
contained could not be met when God is the agent. Hence,
such principles are unable to make a logically necessary connection between either kind of evil and the non-existence of
God. Philosophers do not seem to have proposed principles
precisely about kinds of evil. It is unlikely that a satisfactory
principle can be found.

For these reasons, the conclusion about kinds of evil is
this:

It seems impossible to show that the existence of God is
incompatible with each kind of evil.

If this conclusion could not be drawn, further questions
about degrees and multiple instances of evil would be
excluded absolutely. Since it can be drawn, at least with
respect to a single instance of each kind of evil in some
degree, enquiry may be made about other degrees and multiple instances of each kind of actual evil. These problems
will be discussed together since the same sort of arguments
apply in each case.

About Degrees and Multiplicity of Evil

Is the existence of God compatible with every degree and
multiplicity of actual evil?

No direct argument about this can be given. We cannot
state what degrees of evil or how many instances of each
degree occur. Nor do we know what good is logically

possible and whether it could justify them. Consequently, we cannot suggest, for each instance of evil, what proportionate good, if any, would justify the evil.

However, an indirect argument can be given similar to that about kinds of evil. It is this:

> The notion 'good' does not itself exclude the possibility either that what instantiates it should, logically, suppose each of the degrees or multiple instances of actual evil, or that the good should be proportionate to the evil. Therefore, it does not seem possible to show positively that God could not be morally justified in not preventing each of the degrees or multiple instances of actual evil.[9]

This conclusion is confirmed when the problems are examined by the second method. Since there is no direct contradiction in asserting that omnipotent goodness exists in God and that certain degrees or multiple instances of evil exist in other beings, to show that the statements are logically incompatible, a principle must be found which entails the non-existence of God if certain degrees or multiple instances of evil exist.

In arguing from evil to the non-existence of God, philosophers have not usually distinguished the general problem from problems about kinds, degrees and multiple instances of evil. But, they clearly believe that the principles they use apply in all cases of evil. In examining the general problem, implicit or explicit principles suggested by Epicurus, Augustine, Hume, Mackie and Bradley were shown to be simply false. Hence, they must fail with the specific abstract problems as well. An analytically true principle about evil in general was constructed but found to be unsatisfactory. We will now see whether a similar principle about degrees and multiplicity of evil can succeed. This principle will be:

> A being which is able but not willing to prevent certain degrees and multiple instances of evil is malevolent, unless the being is justified in not preventing the evil.

Although analytically true, this principle, on its own, does not make the required logically necessary connection for it leaves undecided whether they are instances of evil which it is logically impossible to justify, with respect to God. Can it be shown that there are such instances? There are only two ways in which this could be done: either by showing that there are degrees and multiplicity of evil which no agent could be justified in not preventing, or by showing that the conditions, in God's case, for justifying the instances of evil could not be met. It will now be asked whether human agents can be justified in not preventing even the worst degrees of evil and multiple instances of it.[10] First, with regard to degrees of evil:

All degrees of moral evil in the future could be prevented if everyone avoided having children.[11] We do not believe that human beings are malevolent because they do not do this. We would not consider that anyone who was able to persuade mankind to do it and did not do so was morally evil. We do not believe that each person is morally obliged to do it himself and to persuade as many as he can to follow him. Accordingly, we recognize limits to an agent's moral obligation to prevent the evil he can prevent, even if it is very great moral evil. He can be morally justified in not preventing it.

As far as physical evil is concerned, there seem to be no degrees of it which a good being always prevents. Many people regard death as the greatest physical evil. We do not consider that those who favour capital punishment are necessarily evil. Nor do we call evil those who could prevent the exercise of capital punishment but do not do so, e.g. Government ministers, trial judges or prison authorities. Again, many people believe that there are other cases in which they are morally free to take the life of another, e.g. when it is the only way to save their own life which is being unjustly threatened, or when their country is under attack in war. There could be circumstances, too, when someone, without blame, failed to prevent serious and permanent injuries to another, e.g. when the alternative was to disclose the whereabouts of Jewish families intended for liquidation,

It does not seem to be true, then, that there are certain degrees of physical evil which no good being could be justified in not preventing. No matter what the physical evil, it seems there could be instances in which a being was justified in not preventing it and will not be evil if he does not do so.

Finally it does not seem to be true that any good being must prevent certain degrees of psychological evil. One of the worst degrees of this evil is torture. Nevertheless, someone can be morally justified in not preventing it even though he could do so. Failure to prevent it might save someone's life, his own or another's. Again, many people consider that to betray one's country by giving vital information to an enemy, rather than to endure torture or allow another to be tortured, is a serious failure in duty and that a person can be justified in permitting even such an extreme psychological evil. It seems then that an agent who does not prevent certain degrees of psychological evil is not necessarily malevolent.

It is not possible to specify all degrees of moral and non-moral evil. It seems, however, that the claim that no agent can be justified in not preventing certain of these cannot succeed with any of them since it fails with some of the worst degrees.

Secondly, with regard to multiple instances of evil:

It was just seen that although there is a way in which all instances of moral and human non-moral evil could be prevented in the future (namely, if people avoided all children), we do not believe there is a moral obligation to use it. Again, we do not always consider evil those who do not prevent multiple evil when they resist foreign troops attempting to overrun their country. Multiple cases of physical evil would be avoided if motor-cars and aeroplanes were banned. We do not think Governments have a moral obligation to ban them. In these cases, and others like them, we admit that human agents can be justified in not preventing multiple instances of moral and non-moral evil.

It seems, then, that it is impossible to show that no agent can be morally justified in not preventing certain degrees and multiple instances of evil. But can it be shown that the conditions, in God's case, for justifying the evil could never be met? It does not seem possible to show this. The conditions would be similar to those given about moral and non-moral evil in the chapter on the general problem, i.e. that there should be proportionate good which could not, logically, be achieved without actual evil. If such good is possible, actual evil could be justified with respect to God. To establish the negative fact that such good is impossible, it would be necessary to have an exhaustive knowledge of possible good and its logical connection, if any, with actual evil. We lack this knowledge. Accordingly, it seems impossible to show, with logical necessity, that actual evil could not be justified with respect to God.

The examples used in the foregoing discussion deserve further emphasis. They show that we believe there are goods so valuable that, in order to have them, we are justified in not preventing some of the worst instances of moral and non-moral evil. It may be that there are goods so valuable that, in order to bring them about, God could be justified in not preventing even the worst cases of evil. In His case, evil would need to be a logically necessary condition of the goods. Although the examples used do not show that there are goods of this kind, they do show that if such goods are possible, the existence of great evil would not, of itself, give logically cogent grounds for rejecting the existence of God.[12] The chapter has claimed that it does not seem possible to show that such goods are logically impossible. If this is the case, it is not possible to show that the world's evil of itself entails the non-existence of God.[13]

NOTES

[1] It is supposed here that discussion of God and evil begins with the traditional problem. If it begins with the specific problems, there will be a third connection, mentioned in a subsequent note (Ch. 5, p. 76, n. 7).

[2] Certain arguments in this chapter will make use of our knowledge of the actual world, but it does not follow that the arguments necessarily depend on matters of fact or that no other arguments are possible. In this, the abstract problems differ from the concrete problems.

3 They say:

It should be clear that the problem we raise is not one of formal inconsistency. We are not claiming that the following statements constitute an inconsistent set: God is almighty, God is all-knowing, God is infinitely good and evil created by this being exists in the finite world. To state the problem in this way begs the real question at issue, namely, whether or not the evil which is plainly evident is gratuitous or serves some purpose and ignores the fact that some evil obviously serves good ends which could not otherwise be achieved. The very possibility of stating the problem of evil as a formal contradiction depends upon claiming that 'there is no morally sufficient reason for an almighty God to allow any instances of evil' is necessarily true. Moreover, if the problem of evil were stated as a formal contradiction the theist would have no difficulty in rebutting it . . . he only has to show that there is some possible explanation of evil. . . . (*Evil and the Concept of God*, pp. 3–4.)

Here, the question whether evil in fact serves some good purpose, which could not otherwise be achieved, is distinguished from the question whether it is logically possible for it to do so, i.e. the specific concrete problems of evil are distinguished from the specific abstract problems. It seems clear that the authors do not believe it is logically impossible for actual evil to be justified.

4 Pp. 57, 72.

5 Ch. 5, pp. 53–4.

6 This study has classified the kinds of evil in another way as well, i.e. as moral and non-moral. This classification will be used in the arguments about kinds, to forestall the objection that the more specific triple division used here may not be exhaustive.

7 Ch. 3, p. 31.

8 Ch. 3, pp. 31–2.

9 In *The Brothers Karamazov*, Ivan asks Alyosha: 'Imagine that you are creating a fabric of human destiny with the object of making men happy in the end, giving them peace and rest at last, but that it was essential and inevitable to torture to death only one tiny creature—that baby beating its breast with its fist, for instance—and to found that edifice on its tears, would you consent to be architect, on those conditions?' Alyosha replies: 'No, I wouldn't consent' (F. Dostoevski, *The Brothers Karamazov*, trans. C. Garnett, New York, Modern Library Inc., 1950, Bk. V, Ch. 4). Does this, by implication, refute the indirect argument? To a claim that it does, the following points may be made in reply: (i) While there are cases of evil which no one could be justified in causing, it does not follow that no one could be justified in not preventing them. (ii) If someone holds that no one, including God, could be justified in not preventing, e.g. the torture of a baby, he must, logically, also hold that there is, and that for a long time there has been, a moral obligation on all men and women to allow the race to die out as soon as possible in order to prevent every future case of such evil. (iii) It seems untrue that not preventing the torture of a baby might be logically necessary for men to be happy and at

peace. Even if true, it does not follow that the good, logically connected with the evil, could not be proportionate to the evil and justify not preventing it. (iv) Theists, such as Christians, who believe that innocent suffering can have great value, should have less difficulty than others in conceiving that there might be proportionate good logically connected with such evil. (v) In the paragraph preceding the one quoted above, Ivan says that he would maintain his position (one similar to Alyosha's) 'even if (he) were wrong'. This, indeed, can be done but no rational objection to the argument given arises if it is done.

[10] Although the examples which follow are taken from the world as it is, it would be possible, in principle, to draw the same conclusions if the examples were merely imagined and not real. It seems possible, too, to leave aside examples and argue that there is no way of showing that an agent could not, logically, be justified in failing to prevent the evil in question.

[11] Human non-moral evil would be avoided also. As far as animals are concerned, we do not believe human beings are morally obliged to exterminate painlessly all the kinds of animals they can.

[12] John Wisdom agrees. He says: 'It is possible that there is or will be in this world something, say a kingdom of heaven, of so great value, that any world without it would be worse than this one and that further the present evil is a logically necessary condition of it' (*loc. cit.*).

[13] Nor does it seem possible to show that there could be a world containing so much evil that it was logically incompatible with God's existence. We do not seem able to exclude, even in this case, the possibility of justifying good, logically related to the evil, which an omnipotent and omniscient being could bring about. Then, of course, the evil would be off-set by proportionate good.

5

The Concrete Problems

The concrete problems ask whether the conditions under which the existence of God is compatible with actual evil are in fact met. Which evils do these problems concern? They concern every instance of actual evil which needs to be justified. That is to say, they concern every instance of evil which will ever occur.

Possible instances of evil which will never be actual do not concern the concrete problems, for these arise not from the possibility of evil but from its actual occurrence. Actual instances of evil are all of those cases of evil which have existed in the past, which exist now and which will exist in the future. None of them can be excluded from the concrete problems, for if any one sets up a *prima facie* objection to the existence of an infinitely good, omnipotent God, each one does.[1]

It is at once apparent that all of the concrete problems of evil cannot be stated. We do not possess the factual knowledge needed to do this.

About the past, it is impossible for us to list all of the evil which has occurred. There are many reasons for this, e.g. it is very likely that there were examples of evil unknown even when they occurred: these could be both the physical and the psychological evils of beings capable of reflective consciousness who were never, in fact, conscious of them; it is likely that there were instances of evil which were consciously known only to those afflicted; there were probably cases of moral evil known only to the agent either because they affected no one else, or because, although they affected others, the evil derived from the agent's motive or beliefs, or they were not recognized by others as evil; even if all cases of past evil could be known, it would scarcely be possible to list them. Furthermore, it could never be known that all of them were in fact listed.

About the present, all of these points, except the first, apply with a change of tense.

About the future, it must be admitted that we are even less able to list future evils than we are to list present and past ones. Since the future has not occurred, there are as yet no instances of evil to list. But it cannot be assumed that there will be no instances and, if there are, they will raise concrete problems.

Briefly: the concrete problems of evil arise with actual instances of evil, past, present, and future. Since no one knows all of these instances, no one can state all of the problems which they raise.

Does this mean that it is impossible to finally answer all of these problems?[2] What reply is given to this question depends on what is to count as a final answer. If a statement which, in practice, cannot be shown to be true counts as a final answer,[3] such answers may be able to be found to all of the concrete problems of evil. If, however, only statements which are, in practice, capable of being shown to be true count as final answers, such answers cannot be given to all of the problems. To show that the statements are true would be to show, in the case of affirmative answers, that the actual good they refer to does in fact justify all instances of evil and, in the case of negative answers, that no good which justifies all evil will ever exist. Neither of these things can be shown. One reason is that it is impossible to show whether or not each instance of actual evil is justified unless each instance is known.

There is another equally important reason why the concrete problems of evil cannot all be finally answered. In order to finally answer them it would be necessary to know not only all of the evil which will ever occur, but also all of the good which will ever occur for it might justify the evil. It would be necessary to know the good both in itself and in its relation, if any, to the evil. Neither of these things is possible. Good may be past, present or future. It may include the good of the world as a whole, if there is such good, as well as the good of its parts. It may include remote good as well as proximate good. It may include good which contributes to the general welfare of the parts as well as particular good. It may include particular good of all kinds: spiritual, intellectual, ethical, aesthetic, psychological, physical. *A priori*, it cannot be assumed that any of this possible good is not relevant to the justifying of evil and complete knowledge of all of the instances of it which will ever exist is not possible. Because the world is a continuing thing in which people and events influence one another incalculably, it will be even less possible to know the connection, if any, of actual good with actual evil.

Both affirmative and negative answers to the concrete problems of evil which were able to be verified would suppose complete knowledge about actual good and its connection, if any, with evil, and no one has this. Hence, there is a second reason why it is not possible to give definitive answers to all of these problems.

Hitherto, the assumptions of both theist and non-theist seem to have been mistaken. They seem to have taken for granted not only that it should be possible to state all of the concrete problems of evil but also that it should be possible to say what good justifies the evil, if it is in fact justified. Both of these assumptions may be challenged. Perhaps the second assumption rests upon two others commonly made, namely, that the same kind of evil would be justified, if at all, by the same kind of good and that all evil would be justified by one or a few kinds of good only. These assumptions may also be challenged.

There seems to be no reason in principle why instances of evil of the same kind should not be justified in wholly different or partly different ways. Nor does there seem to be any reason, in principle, why two instances of the same kind and degree should not be justified in ways that differ wholly or in part. In practice, when the great diversity of actual evil is taken into account, it seems unlikely that the same good or the same few goods could justify all evil. Consider the variety of kind and degree of evil we know to exist. Moral evil is very different from physical and psychological evil. It is not certain that physical or psychological evil is exactly the same in animals as it is in human beings. Within these general categories, there are vast differences of degree. Lying is morally wrong and so is the betrayal of a friend or murder. The loss of a toe is a physical evil and so is the loss of a leg. Slight pain or suffering is a psychological evil and so is great pain or suffering. Evil can vary, too, in the number of instances of it which occur.

Apart from the diversity of actual evil, there are other facts about it which make it still less likely that all evil could be justified by a few goods only. The things about which it is predicated do not exist in a vacuum but in a context. The full context in which evil occurs is the history of the world. Beings affected by evil are part of a whole which has a history of some thousands of millions of years already and which seems likely to have a very long future. The immediate context in which evil among human beings occurs varies greatly. Human beings differ in background, capacities, needs and the circumstances of their lives. They differ in their activities and interests and in their effect upon other human beings, upon nature and upon events. They have aspects which are not easily discernible, e.g. their religious, ethical and aesthetic values, their virtues and vices, their thought and feeling. These facts seem to make possible a great diversity of good which might justify evil, and they seem to make it improbable that all evil could be justified by either a single kind of good or by several kinds of good only. This, if sound, is a further ground for claiming that all of the concrete problems cannot be solved by us. It is also a ground for claiming that attempted solutions will not even survive objections based on the knowledge of the world we do have.

To state and to answer definitively all of the concrete

problems of evil, a God's-eye view of the world which saw not only everything evil and everything good of the past, the present and the future, but also how they are inter-related would be necessary. This view would need to span the whole history of the world and its final outcome, as a whole and in its parts. If certain theist claims are true, it would need to take into account supernatural facts, the significance of Jesus Christ and the reality and nature of an after-life. Human beings cannot lay claim to omniscience of this kind.

The foregoing discussion shows that theists who attempt to solve all of the concrete problems of evil are mistaken and non-theists who object to their solutions on the ground that they do not succeed are also mistaken. Both assume that, if there are solutions to the problems, they ought to be available to us.

Can at least some of the concrete problems of evil be answered definitively? What is certain is that a negative answer cannot be given to any concrete problem of evil, if it is taken as an independent problem. Such an answer would require knowledge of a negative fact, namely, that no good which justifies the evil will ever exist. No one can know this since all of the good facts about the world cannot be known.

It follows that the existence of God can be positively disproved only through the abstract problems of evil and not through the concrete problems taken as distinct problems. If a negative answer is given to any abstract problem, God's non-existence is entailed, should the evil in question actually exist. Since a negative answer cannot be given to any of the concrete problems, apart from the parallel abstract problem, no answer to these problems as separate problems will ever entail the non-existence of God.

Whether or not an affirmative answer can be given to some concrete problems depends entirely on what facts are available and known. *A priori*, there does not seem to be any good reason why a given problem must be able to be decided here and now. Since both actual evil and actual good are matters of fact, it is impossible to stipulate which instances will occur, when they will occur, or how easily discernible by us they will be. In practice, the answer may depend on which concrete problems are raised. Thus, if it is asked what justifies all instances of physical evil, no answer seems possible for the reasons given already. If it is asked what justifies certain known instances of physical evil, an answer may or may not be possible. It could be that an answer which seems to account for physical evil in general does not wholly account for the particular instances chosen, e.g. very serious cases of physical evil. These instances might be fully justified only through other good which may or may not exist. If it exists, it may or may not be known to us. People who suffer such evil can vary greatly in their personal history, in their future and in their connection with other people and events. It might be that in certain cases circumstances like these are relevant to a full justification of physical evil and that there is no way of knowing them at all or, at least, no guarantee that they are all known. Hence, it may not be possible to show that certain known cases of evil are fully justified if God exists. The only answer available may be an indefinite one. But it may be possible to show that other cases are justified.

Therefore, it is a mistake for theists to attempt to answer all of the concrete problems or to think that they must be able to answer every stated problem. However, theists have tried to provide universal solutions and non-theists have attacked their solutions for failing to show that all evil is in fact justified. The literature on God and evil gives a central place to this debate. Whole books, articles and chapters of books have been written about it.[4] The reason for this interest is plain. The concrete problems concern actual evil in all its instances: moral evils like hatred, injustice, greed; physical evils like illness, injury, loss of limbs; psychological evils like pain. No one is untouched by evil. The total amount of the world's evil is vast. It suggests the questions: If the world was created by a wholly good, omnipotent being, what justifies this evil? Is it in fact justified? Yet, philosophically, the most important problems about God and evil are the abstract problems, not the concrete problems. First, the abstract problems are more fundamental. If it could be shown that the existence of God is, logically, incompatible either with any evil at all or with some existing evil, actual evil could not be justified in any world. The concrete problems would then be excluded radically. The concrete problems arise only because that cannot be shown. Secondly, whether God's existence is compatible with evil does not depend on any matter of fact. Any definitive answer is logically necessary. On the other hand, whether the conditions for compatibility are met is fact-dependent in the sense already explained. These conditions are met only if evil is actually justified, that is, only if good which could justify it does come to exist.[5] This question cannot be solved by purely philosophic means: answers to it depend on facts. But facts need not be available, and in this case they are not.

It remains true, however, that the concrete problems have been treated as if it were, in principle, possible for us to say what justifies evil, if it is justified. Some of the best-known theistic 'solutions' to the concrete problems will now be examined in order to confirm the claim that the nature of the concrete problems makes it impossible for them all to be solved in any way that can be shown to be true. The theories to be examined are those of Leibniz,[6] John Hick, C. A. Campbell and G. H. Joyce, S.J. In each case a brief outline of the theory will be followed by a critical assessment of it.[7]

Leibniz

Leibniz believed that the existence of God can be established independently of evil. Consequently, problems about God and evil are in no way problems about God's existence but problems of how to account for evil since an omnipotent and wholly good God exists. He tried to solve these problems by claiming that all actual evil is a necessary element in the best possible world. Because it is a necessary means to the greatest good, the world's evil is justified.

Leibniz believed that this world is the best world possible, not on empirical but on theoretical grounds. God would make only the best possible world. He was free to create an unlimited variety of world or to create none, but if He created He would make only the best world. No agent acts rationally unless he has a sufficient reason for what he does. Because God is both infinitely wise and good, the only sufficient reason He could have for choosing a world is that the sum of its perfection is the greatest possible.

Were other less good worlds really possible and was God really free to choose this one, since He must act for a sufficient reason? Could there be a sufficient reason for choosing any other world than the best possible? Leibniz's answer is that the creation of this world was not logically or metaphysically necessary but that it was morally necessary and certain to take place: 'One can say in a sense that it is necessary . . . that God should choose what is best . . . But this necessity . . . is not the necessity which I shall call logical, geometric or metaphysical, the denial of which involves a contradiction.'[8]

It is not clear that this reply is satisfactory. No doubt an unlimited number of worlds are logically possible in themselves, but Leibniz needs to explain in what sense it was possible for God to create them. Perhaps he wants to say that, as far as power is concerned, God could have created many different worlds, but that being wholly wise and good as well as omnipotent He would in fact choose only one of these worlds.

In any event, Leibniz's main claim that in making this world, God must have made the best possible world, remains intact. An obvious argument against it is the existence of evil. Leibniz does not attempt to deny its existence. He says that evil contributes to the world's perfection in such a way that, without it, the world would not be the best possible. The reason is that 'the best alternative is not always that which tends to avoid evil, since it can happen that evil may be accompanied by a greater good':[9] and 'Not only does (God) derive from (evils) greater goods, but He finds them connected with the greatest goods of all those that are possible; so that it would be a fault not to permit them.'[10]

For Leibniz, then, the best possible world is not a perfect

world, that is, a world free of all imperfection. It must contain the evil which the present world had in the past, does have now, and will have in the future for without it a world which, taken as a whole, is the best possible, would not exist. Consequently, the answer to all of the concrete problems of evil, as Leibniz understands them, is that in every case, actual evil is a necessary means to greater good and, ultimately, to the greatest good.

The first serious objection to this theory is that it depends on prior acceptance of the existence of an omnipotent, wholly good God. It lacks all force for anyone who is not convinced that God's existence can be firmly established despite actual evil. If his proofs of God's existence are rejected, Leibniz has no argument to offer for the claim that this is the best possible world. Could the best possible world be recognized? Leibniz gives no sufficient criterion for recognizing it and it does not seem possible to give one.[11] Similarly, his claim that every actual evil is a necessary means to greater good is unable to be verified. His main ground for the claim is that since God exists it must be true. Once God's existence is not assumed or accepted, the claim must fail. The chief reasons for this were set out earlier: we can know neither all of the world's evil nor all of the world's good which might justify it. It is therefore impossible to verify that in every case actual evil is a necessary means to greater good.

The most radical objection to Leibniz's theory is that 'the best possible world' is a meaningless expression which refers to no possible world. Leibniz believes that one universe is more perfect than another if it has a greater variety and richness of beings in it. The best world is the one which has the greatest variety and richness possible. Without evil, certain beings or certain perfections of beings could not exist, and that is the reason why evil must exist. All actual evil is needed if this world is to be the one of 'most reality, most perfection, most significance'.[12]

It is possible to decide on a criterion for 'the best possible world' and then find it realized in only one world. However, in using the phrase 'the best possible world', Leibniz seems to mean a world which is best absolutely, that is, a world whose perfection cannot, logically, be surpassed. Such a world does not seem possible. According to Leibniz's prescription, it would need to contain the greatest possible variety of beings. Does it make sense to speak of the greatest possible variety of trees, flowers, fish, animals, human character, art, music? It seems that no matter what variety should exist a still greater variety would be logically possible. In this respect, 'the best possible world' is like 'the biggest possible world' or 'the longest possible line'. All of these seem to be pseudo-concepts. No matter how large a world was, a larger would seem conceivable. No matter how varied a world was, a more varied world seems able to be conceived.

Perhaps Leibniz envisages an infinite number of worlds which, if they were all actual, would leave no other world to come into existence. If this were logically possible, it would be at least plausible to say that one of the worlds was more perfect and richer than any of the others. But it does not seem to be logically possible. 'Infinite' has two senses. In one sense it applies to what is unlimited and always fully actual. The only example of this seems to be God Himself. In the other sense, it applies to whatever can increase indefinitely but can never be fully actual. To say that the number of possible worlds is infinite is to say that the number of worlds can grow indefinitely, endlessly. Whatever the mathematical concept of infinity may be and whether it refers to anything which, logically, could exist, does not affect the matter. No matter how many worlds actually existed a greater number seems logically possible. The same thing seems to apply to the notion of a varied and rich world. No matter what variety of beings a world should have, and consequently, no matter how rich a world should be, it seems logically possible that a more varied and richer world should exist. If this is so, a world which is, absolutely, the best is no possible world, and Leibniz's notion is a pseudo-notion. If this argument is considered inconclusive, the meaningfulness of 'the best possible world' will be doubtful. This is sufficient to make Leibniz's whole theory doubtful. If it is thought that the argument is unsound and that 'the best possible world', in Leibniz's sense, is not meaningless, it will remain true that it is impossible to verify that each instance of evil is a logically necessary condition of greater good.[13] The theory cannot avoid being unsatisfactory on that ground once God's existence is not accepted.

John Hick

John Hick's theory can be summarized in the following six points:

(1) God's purpose in creating this world was to provide the logically necessary environment in which human persons could respond freely to His infinite love and freely accept a God-centred rather than a self-centred life. Such a world is better than a world without evil, or a world with less evil but with morally determined beings.[14]

(2) The freedom needed by human beings if they are to respond to God as free persons and not as automata logically supposes an element of unpredictability which makes it impossible for God to ensure that moral evil will never occur.[15]

(3) Pain and suffering are part of the environment logically necessary for the moral growth of persons by trial and testing.[16]

(4) The apparently excessive pain and suffering in the world is due partly to its being the necessary condition of certain virtues and partly to the positive value of mystery which challenges faith and trust.[17]

(5) The joys of life after death will amply compensate for the difficulties of this life and there will be no human being who does not have them.[18]

(6) The existence of animals which will suffer pain is explained by their being a necessary part of an environment which sets men at a distance from God so that no one is compelled to accept Him: their pain is compensated for by animal good.[19]

This theory shares with every theory which attempts to justify all evil, the disadvantage that there is no way of knowing whether it is true. Even when Christian belief is taken into account, it cannot be shown with certainty what God's exact plan for the whole world may be. Accordingly, Hick cannot show that he has correctly outlined it. It is, of course, impossible to verify the success of any suggested plan.

Secondly, for Hick, the moral choices required by God's purpose for the world are, in part, unpredictable, which seems to mean that even God cannot know what they will be until they have been made. If this is so, it is difficult to see how He could know in advance that His purpose will in fact be achieved with good results. How could God be certain, before creating, that a free response to the good would be made in even one case or at least in enough cases to justify the world's evil? Uncertainty about the good outcome of the world makes it doubtful whether God was justified in creating. The risk seems too great. Furthermore, although he believes that all men, no matter how evil in this world, will share the blessedness of an after-life, Hick gives no clear ground for certainty of this. If unforced moral response to God and to good is a supreme value, it is difficult to see how it could be certain, either before creation or after it, that all men will actually make this response in this life or in the next. For his belief Hick claims not absolute certainty but practical certainty because of God's power to win people to Himself. However, he does not explain how this power of God's is to be reconciled with unforced moral responses in every instance.

If God had foreknowledge of the outcome of the world, Hick's theory would be more plausible. God might know when creating that the number, kind and degree of instances of authentically free moral response would be of such intrinsic value as to outweigh all actual evil. He might also foresee that because people and events are connected, it would do more harm than good in the long run to prevent certain evils miraculously. Hick's appeal to mystery might be accepted too. One term of the concrete problems of evil is an infinite and transcendent God. Our finite rational intelligences incline to reject whatever cannot be reduced to our thought categories. The unclearness of mystery could be a necessary condition of our responding adequately to God. Worship, for example, supposes inequality of a radical kind which excludes the making of demands even for clarity. It supposes total submission and trust. A response of this kind might not be possible without mystery. However, as it stands, Hick's theory cannot be explained in this way. Even if it could, it would still be impossible to verify the theory.

There are other difficulties for the theory as an explanation of all actual evil. The theory rests on the unprovable assumption that the world as it exists at any moment is logically necessary for the kind of perfection which God wants to be possible. The theory requires that every evil should be logically related to this perfection and, indeed, logically necessary for this perfection. It is hard to see how this can be. There was a great deal of physical and psychological evil among animals before human beings appeared at all. It is not clear how all of this was logically necessary for the possibility of moral growth among human beings. Once men appeared, there has been a great deal of the same evil in parts of the world uninhabited by humans. It is not clear how this was logically necessary for the possibility of authentic moral growth. The theory must be modified in some way to account for evils like these.

Hick admits that his theory cannot clearly answer all objections to it.[20] He does not seem to realize, however, that a universal theory capable of proof is not possible. If it is not possible, theists cannot be expected to give it.

C. A. Campbell

C. A. Campbell divides evil into moral evil and suffering,[21] offering a different solution in each case. His solution to moral evil is extremely simple. Like Hick he believes that God intends the world to be a place for 'soul-making' but, unlike Hick, he thinks that God may intend other things as well. Soul-making, or the achieving of moral values, cannot occur unless human beings have free will which 'is meaningless if it is not a freedom to choose *wrongly* as well as *rightly*'.[22] If free will exists, a world without moral evil is not conceivable.[23]

Campbell considers one difficulty against his theory, namely that the suffering caused by moral evil to the innocent is so great that the world would be better if free will did not exist at all. He believes that, in the end, this is an argument against the existence of God and of certain forms of suffering, not an argument about moral evil and God.[24]

There are several objections to the theory. First, while it is clear that free will among human beings in a finite world seems to make moral evil always possible, it is not clear that it need make moral evil ever necessary. The concept of a human being who freely chooses good always does not seem to be a contradictory one. Human beings as they now are never seem to avoid evil completely, but it seems logically possible for God to have made human nature so that virtue was easy. Would even this have guaranteed sinlessness, if human beings were self-determining or if the world was an evolutionary one? No, but it seems possible for an omnipotent and omniscient being to have made only those who would in fact always avoid evil and to have made a non-evolving world. Campbell does not show that this is not possible. If it is, his theory does not account adequately for moral evil.[25]

Secondly, even if it is true that free will cannot exist without moral evil, this does not entail that all of the moral evil which occurs is necessary. Campbell's theory, if true, would justify only some moral evil, not all of it. Why could God not have chosen a world of free beings who were guilty of some moral evil, but of much less moral evil than we are? This seems possible for an omniscient being.

Thirdly, if it is the case that all actual moral evil is both unavoidable and justified by greater moral goodness, there is no way of showing it.

Finally, the objection outlined by Campbell does not seem able to be reduced to a problem about suffering. The objection concerns suffering brought about through moral evil. It seems possible for God to have created a world of free beings who would not have been guilty of those moral faults which lead to the instances of suffering with which the objection deals. Campbell does not explain why God has not done this.

As for suffering, Campbell believes that there is no problem for theists in deserved suffering, e.g. when a wrong-doer is punished.[26] Neither does all undeserved suffering create a problem. Some of it is a necessary condition for the highest moral virtue.[27] The undeserved suffering which Campbell considers a problem for theists is that which is 'immoderate in degree' and 'long protracted'.[28] He seems uncertain what solution to this problem he wants to propose. At one place he casts doubt on the solution that the advantages of a law-governed universe would be lost if God intervened to prevent all suffering of great degree and duration, asking whether God could not have so constructed human beings that they would be incapable of experiencing such suffering.[29] Later, he suggests combining this solution, in a way he does not define, with another, namely, that the joys of life after death will amply compensate for all suffering.[30] But, against this, he puts the objection that God could confer these joys without the suffering, and in the best conceivable world, the only one which a perfect being would create, this would be done.[31] The answer to the objection which he accepts tentatively is his final answer to the problem of intense and prolonged, undeserved suffering. It is that even this kind of suffering may be a necessary condition for the highest moral achievement.[32]

The first objection to this theory is that whether or not deserved suffering creates a problem depends on whether Campbell's solution to moral evil is acceptable. If it is unacceptable, there will be cases of moral evil which have gone unjustified. Those punished for this evil will undergo deserved suffering in Campbell's sense, but it too will be unjustified and therefore a problem. Several reasons for questioning his solution to moral evil have been given.

Secondly, it is doubtful that no instance of undeserved suffering which is neither intense nor long causes a problem. There are probably many cases in which this suffering does not lead to virtue. If God has foreknowledge of them, it can be asked why he did not make a world in which this kind of suffering would always be used as a means to virtue.

Thirdly, his final solution to the problem of intense, prolonged, undeserved suffering cannot be shown to be true in every instance or in any instance of such suffering. Unless it is true in every instance, a similar problem to that just mentioned will arise.

Fourthly, Campbell's theory says nothing at all about certain kinds of evil, e.g. the loss of limbs in men or animals, or suffering in animals.

Fifthly, his apparent acceptance of Leibniz's notion of 'the best possible world' can be questioned.

G. H. Joyce, S.J.

G. H. Joyce, S.J., believes that free will does not entail wrong-doing either because a being can be free and yet incapable of doing wrong, as in the case of the Blessed in Heaven, or because God can give such strength and guidance in this world that, while remaining free, no one ever misuses his freedom.[33] His answer to the problem of moral evil is that, on the one hand, it is better for us to merit beatitude than to receive it gratuitously and that, on the other, the meriting of it supposes that moral failure is genuinely possible.[34] He considers the difficulty that God could have made a world in which failure was always possible but never in fact occurred. His final answer to it is that if this happened 'the perversity of the creature would have prevailed over the goodness of the Creator, and human wickedness would have compelled God to modify His purposes . . . It belongs to God to determine His designs with perfect goodness, but in supreme independence of creatures.'[35] Joyce also holds that moral evil in some people is a means to moral growth in others and that the attaining of moral perfection is a good which outweighs the evil.[36]

He concludes: 'The existence of moral evil must ever remain the greatest of the world's mysteries: and it is idle to imagine that we can remove entirely the difficulty we feel in its regard.'[37]

The chief objection to this theory is the one Joyce considers, namely, whether it was not possible for God to have made a world in which everyone would merit beatitude through trial and testing and no one would ever sin. Joyce's reply does not seem satisfactory. The core of his argument is that if God had made such a world He would have been determined by creatures. In the first place, this argument is not expressed accurately. Before creation, there could be question only of possible creatures. It is not easy to see in what sense possible creatures could or could not determine choices. Perhaps what Joyce means is simply that God foresaw that if certain beings came to exist, they would do wrong. Secondly, the element of independence of God which self-determining beings have is God-given. Consequently, neither the bad nor the good use of liberty can be opposed to God's status as Creator. Thirdly, it seems entirely right that if God makes self-determining beings, He takes into account how they will use their liberty. In so far as He is omnipotent, He can act without considering this, but in so far as He is wholly good He will not act independently of the consequences of His actions. Because He is wholly good, there are certain possible states of affairs He will not want to bring about. In this, it is His goodness rather than the states of affairs which determine Him. Fourthly, if Joyce's argument were correct, it would be compatible with His power and goodness for God to make a world in which freedom always caused more harm than good.

It seems, then, that Joyce has not satisfactorily answered the main objection to his theory about moral evil. If a world of free beings who never misuse their freedom is logically possible, and he contends that it is, Joyce has not explained why God has not chosen it.

Secondly, it is impossible to show that the moral failure of some people is always a means and, *a fortiori*, that it is always a logically necessary means, for the moral growth of others. Similarly, it is impossible to show that, taken as a whole, moral achievement outweighs moral evil. Joyce admits that his theory does not answer every difficulty, but does not indicate which difficulties it fails to answer. This will be a major one: that, even if the theory were true, it cannot be shown to be true.

With regard to suffering, Joyce notes that the amount of it in the world's history has been immense. He considers animal suffering first. His solution to it contains the following elements:

(1) Animal suffering is probably far less severe than suffering among humans.[38]

(2) Their pleasures greatly outweigh their pains.[39]

(3) Both pleasure and pain are natural for sentient life; absolute immunity from pain is possible but it would require continual interference with nature.[40]

(4) Pain has some very good results, e.g. hunger impels an animal to search for food and so preserve its life.[41]

(5) Carnivorism is accounted for chiefly by the fact that, apart from man, the perfection of creation as a whole, not in its parts, is intended by God. What is evil for one species is good for another.[42]

Joyce's solution to human suffering uses several of these elements, e.g. that happiness outweighs unhappiness.[43] However, the main part of his solution is that physical evil is a necessary condition for moral progress by personal effort.[44]

Against Joyce's solution to animal suffering, at least two chief objections can be made. First, it does not seem to be certain that a necessary part of the nature of any sentient being is to feel pain as well as pleasure. Sentient beings which can naturally feel pleasure but not pain seem conceivable. It seems possible, too, that pain could achieve its good effects more readily and more often. Secondly, there is no way of showing that the sum of animal pleasure in the world's history outweighs the sum of animal suffering. It does not seem always to do so in individual cases.

Similar points can be made about Joyce's subsidiary arguments in the case of human suffering. His main argument leaves unexplained instances in which suffering does not seem to lead to moral progress. Finally, it is impossible to show that all suffering is a necessary condition for moral progress or that the amount of moral progress which occurs is proportionate to the amount of actual evil.

An Assessment of the Problems

This brief study of four of the better-known attempts to give complete solutions to the concrete problems of evil has shown that each theory is defective in certain distinctive ways and, in addition, that all of the theories share the defect that none can be shown to be true. As we have seen, the former contention is likely to be true and the latter will certainly be true of any theory which tries to solve all of the problems. We can know neither all of the world's evil, all of the world's good, nor the connections, if any, between the good and the evil. Hence, it will never be possible to devise a theory to justify all evil which can be shown to be true. Given the vast range and context of evil and good, actual and possible, it is unlikely that any theory which, though incapable of proof, can answer every objection raised against it, will ever be devised. This study of four theories has strongly confirmed these claims about the concrete problems of evil.

It follows, as a corollary, that non-theist philosophers who write as if theists should be able to solve all of the concrete problems, if there is any solution to them, are mistaken. It is no argument against theism that it is unable to do what cannot be done. A very recent critical study is Madden and Hare's.[45] These authors devote their entire book to the concrete problems. Some of the lines of argument they use were already well exploited by other writers like J. L. Mackie[46] and H. J. McCloskey.[47] Each of these philosophers shows convincingly that none of the solutions theists commonly offer satisfactorily solves all of the problems. However, if the claim made here about the concrete problems is correct, their whole project along with that of theists who try to offer universal and definitive solutions to all actual evil is misconceived. Both the ingenuity of theists in proposing solutions and the skill of non-theists in rejecting them are misplaced. The nature of the problems makes it impossible for any theist to show that all actual evil is justified.[48]

But it is also true that the nature of these problems makes it impossible for non-theists to show that actual evil is not justified. Usually, non-theists attempt only to show that proposed solutions fail (as they must if they are universal). But it will not then follow that the world's evil is not justified; it will merely follow that no satisfactory account of what justifies it has been given. To show that actual evil is not justified, it would be necessary to establish a negative fact, namely, that good which could justify it will never exist. This cannot be done without exhaustive knowledge of the world's good, which is not available to us. Consequently, there can be and ought to be substantial agreement between theist and non-theist about the concrete problems. They can and should agree that, if the problems are considered on their own, it cannot be shown whether or not actual evil is justified and that the world's evil is not a decisive ground for rejecting the existence of God.

While agreeing that it is not possible to give final answers to all of the concrete problems because, for example, we do not know them, some philosophers may think that it should be possible to give answers to many of those we do know. Perhaps they overlook certain relevant facts about the world and about ourselves. The universe in which evil occurs is very ancient and very complex. We have only recently begun to understand something of its structure, constitution, laws and history. We know little about the origin of life and its development over thousands of years. We can only guess at the future of the world. About its evil or its good we can make only very general and inadequate statements. We have no clear idea how human life is affected by sociological, political, economic, creative, personal and other factors. We cannot assess the effects of human thought and decision, especially on the grand scale in which these occur. We cannot trace the interplay of human actions. Future good and evil is outside our grasp still more: there is no agreement among philosophers on the possibility of life after death.

Besides these facts about the world, there are facts about any philosopher who examines the concrete problems which are also relevant. A philosopher begins his study at a particular point of time. His own history in the world has been short and his future will be limited. He cannot stand outside time and assess the world's good and evil.

When both of these sets of facts are considered, it seems clear that there are solid reasons why we may not be able to show whether or not the evil we know is in fact justified. The issues involved are too complex and too unclear. It does not follow, however, that we cannot give a satisfactory account of any selected instances of evil. We may be able to do this.

Thus, the theories just discussed and other similar ones may shed some light on the concrete problems. Leibniz, for example, seems to be correct in laying it down that all actual evil can be justified only if it is a necessary means to greater good. Hick, Campbell and Joyce may easily be right in claiming that there are instances of evil which are in fact justified because they are the logically necessary condition of unforced moral growth. Similarly, the claim that a good deal of non-moral evil is justified because it is an unavoidable result of the laws of nature which, on the whole, are beneficial, may also be correct. Any acceptable solution will be valuable for it will illustrate how actual evil can be justified. We may also be able to suggest what goods could be relevant to the justifying of certain cases or classes of evil, e.g. Christians may suggest supernatural goods like Heaven, Grace, discipleship of Jesus Christ. But the nature of the concrete problems makes it impossible to predict what success such attempts will have.

These are some of the limited goals a philosopher may put before himself in studying the concrete problems. He may look for full or partial solutions to some of them or to certain classes of them. But, in view of the objections raised against each part of the theories discussed in the previous chapter, and in view of the complexity of the issues, he will have little hope of substantial success.

Another important task of the philosopher will be to examine suggested solutions to see what problems, if any, they solve. What the philosopher cannot do, however, is to show positively that there will never be satisfactory solutions to all of the problems. In their book, Madden and Hare do not claim that they can do this. They argue that unless evil which is *prima facie* gratuitous can be shown to be actually necessary for good, there will be a good reason, although not a sufficient reason, for rejecting theism. This seems to be certainly true if the concrete problems are considered on their own. Since it is not possible to show that all actual evil is justified,[49] it may never be justified. This is clearly, in itself, a good reason for rejecting theism. On the other hand, it is not a sufficient reason, for the logical impossibility of all actual evil being justified eventually cannot be shown. Hence, actual evil would give a sufficient reason for rejecting theism only if it could be shown that the abstract problems must be answered negatively, but this does not seem able to be done. On that fact theists must be content to insist.

The theist has sound reasons for insisting on it. When there is question of human agents only, we put little weight upon what is merely logically possible. Often human agents do not know what is logically possible or, if they do, they either cannot bring it about or are unlikely to do so. The problems with which this study has been concerned, however, are not only problems about evil, they are also problems about a being who is wholly good and omnipotent. If God exists, there exists an omniscient being who knows everything that it is logically possible for unlimited power to achieve and how to achieve it; an omnipotent being exists which has unlimited power; a wholly good being exists which will bring about whatever omnipotence can bring about to justify evil. A theist may rightly point out the consistency of this position. It suggests, however, a new reason why it may not be possible for us to go very far in solving the concrete problems. We have very imperfect knowledge of the logically possible. Consequently, what God, if He exists, is able and intends to achieve through the world and its evil may not be apparent to us in most cases of evil.

Accordingly, the only positive answer that can now be given to the concrete problems is an indirect one, i.e. the answer that all actual evil is justified if God exists.

NOTES

[1] It might be argued that since all instances or at least many instances of evil can be classified according to kind, the term 'concrete problems of evil' should rather be used of the kinds of instances than of every instance of each kind. However, evil differs not only in kind but also in degree and multiplicity so that there is no sure way of grouping together instances of evil which raise precisely the same problem. Even if there were, it would still be uncertain whether each group of instances would be justified, if at all, by the same good. These points will be developed later in this section.

'Actual evil' and 'actual good' are used in a technical sense and refer to every instance of evil or good which will ever be actual.

[2] In this study a necessary condition for an answer being final or definitive is that it is either a negative or an affirmative answer. An indefinite answer is excluded.

[3] The statement may be able to be shown to be false or meaningless, of course. For example, it will be argued soon that Leibniz's theory that all actual evil is necessary in the best possible world is meaningless. Only a negative or affirmative answer which can be shown to be true, apart from independent proof of God's existence, will be considered final or definitive. If God's existence were proved independently, it would follow that actual evil is in fact justified even if we do not know which good justifies it. (Of course, philosophers who hold that all justification theories are mistaken will reject this. Whether a proof of God's existence is possible will not be investigated. It will not be assumed that it is possible.

[4] E.g. Augustine, *Confessions*, Bk. VII, Chs. 3–5, 12–16; *Enchiridion*,

Chs. 3–5; Leibniz, *Theodicy*; Hume, *op. cit.*; A. D. Sertillanges, *op. cit.*; Jacques Maritain, *St Thomas and the Problem of Evil*, Milwaukee, Marquette University Press, 1942; *God and the Permission of Evil*, trans. Joseph W. Evans, Milwaukee, the Bruce Publishing Co., 1965; J. L. Mackie, *op. cit.*; H. J. McCloskey, *op. cit.*; John Hick, *op. cit.*; Antony Flew, 'Divine Omnipotence and Human Freedom', *New Essays in Philosophical Theology*, ed. by A. Flew and A. MacIntyre, New York, the Macmillan Co., 1955; *God and Philosophy*, London, Hutchinson & Co., 1966, pp. 48–57; Charles Journet, *The Meaning of Evil*, London, Geoffrey Chapman, 1963; C. A. Campbell, *On Selfhood and Godhood*, London, Allen & Unwin Ltd., 1957; G. H. Joyce, S.J., *Principles of Natural Theology*, London, Longmans, Green, 3rd edn. 1957.

5 As stated already, if the conditions are met it will not follow that God does exist: it will only follow that He could exist despite evil. Positive proofs of God's existence lie outside the scope of this study.

6 Although Leibniz does not deal with the concrete problems in the direct way that Hick and others do, his is implicitly a theory about the concrete problems proposed as true. It is also a classical theory. For these reasons it will be examined here.

7 In proposing solutions to the concrete problems, these writers implicitly propose solutions to the traditional problem. If any actual evil is justified the traditional problem is necessarily solved. As well, they implicitly propose solutions to the specific abstract problems about actual evil. If actual evil is in fact justified, it follows necessarily that it is logically possible for it to be justified.

8 *Theodicy, Essays on the Goodness of God, the Freedom of Man and the Origin of Evil*, trans. E. M. Huggard, London, Routledge & Kegan Paul, 1952, 282.

9 *Op. cit.*, Summary.

10 *Op. cit.*, 127.

11 Of course, even if such a criterion could be given, it would be impossible to verify that all actual evil is necessary for the best possible world.

12 *Op. cit.*, 201.

13 Or of the greatest good, i.e. of the best possible world.

14 *Evil and the God of Love*, pp. 290–7, 307–11.

15 *Ibid.*, pp. 310–12, 379.

16 *Ibid.*, pp. 360–3.

17 *Ibid.*, pp. 369–72.

18 *Ibid.*, pp. 378–81, 386–8.

19 *Ibid.*, pp. 351–3.

20 *Op. cit.*, p. 369.

21 Strictly, Campbell says '. . . the problem of *natural* evil, which it is customary to identify, more or less accurately, with the problem of *suffering*' (*op. cit.*, p. 272, his italics).

22 *Op. cit.*, p. 274 (his italics).

23 *Ibid.*, p. 275.

24 *Ibid.*, p. 275.

25 See Ninian Smart, 'Omnipotence, Evil and Supermen', *Philosophy*, Vol. XXXVI, No. 137 (1961); Antony Flew, 'Are Ninian Smart's Temptations Irresistible?' *Philosophy*, Vol. XXXVII, No. 139 (1962); J. L. Mackie, 'Theism and Utopia', *Philosophy*, Vol. XXXVII, No. 139 (1962).

26 *Ibid.*, p. 287.

27 *Ibid.*, p. 288.

28 *Ibid.*, p. 288.

29 *Ibid.*, pp. 299–300.

30 *Ibid.*, pp. 301–3.

31 *Ibid.*, p. 303.

32 *Ibid.*, pp. 303–4.

33 (*Op. cit.*, p. 600.) Ninian Smart has maintained that the belief that God could have created a world of wholly good men depends for its plausibility on the theory that free will and causal determinism are compatible. Furthermore, he argues that even if this theory is accepted, it is unclear whether it would make sense to speak of such men as good because, e.g. 'good' is said of beings which are liable to temptation (*op. cit.*). It seems that Joyce would dispute the view that the notion of a world of wholly good men relies upon the compatibility of free will and determinism. If it is possible for someone to determine himself to good, despite temptation, on some occasions, it seems possible for him to do this on every occasion, provided that God ensures that his strength of will and mind does not fail. Whether God could make a world of self-determining beings of this kind who always would choose the good, depends on whether it is possible for God to have foreknowledge of such choices. If this is possible, as Joyce seems to think, there is no reason why these beings should not be called 'good'.

34 *Ibid.*, pp. 600–1.

35 *Ibid.*, pp. 601–2.

36 *Ibid.*, pp. 603–4.

37 *Ibid.*, p. 606.

38 *Ibid.*, pp. 585–6.

39 *Ibid.*, p. 586.

40 *Ibid.*, p. 587.

41 *Ibid.*, p. 587.

42 *Ibid.*, pp. 588–92.

43 *Ibid.*, p. 593.

44 *Ibid.*, pp. 593–8.

45 *Evil and the Concept of God.*

46 'Evil and Omnipotence', *Mind*, Vol. LXIV (1955).

47 'God and Evil', *Philosophical Quarterly*, Vol. X, No. 39 (1960).

48 That is, it is not possible to show this when the question of God and evil is considered on its own. If God's existence could be established independently of evil, it would follow that all actual evil is in fact justified. However, this would not be accepted by anyone who rejects every justification theory.

49 I.e. apart from positive proofs of God's existence, independent of evil.

Conclusion

There are two general conclusions from this study:

(1) Apart from positive proofs of God's existence, it cannot be shown that the world's evil is logically compatible with the existence of a wholly good, omnipotent being, or that the conditions for compatibility are in fact met.

(2) It cannot be shown that the world's evil is logically incompatible with God's existence, or that the conditions for compatibility are not in fact met.

But, it may be argued that although it cannot be shown that there is a logically necessary connection between evil and the non-existence of God, it may be possible to show that there is a synthetically necessary connection between them. We saw that such a connection cannot be established by means of the principles used by Epicurus, Augustine, Hume and others. Perhaps it can be established by other principles, e.g. a good being always prevents suffering to innocent children. It might be argued that such principles are *synthetic a priori* principles and necessarily true.

Strictly speaking, this view does not come within the scope of the present study. It involves questions such as the notion of *synthetic a priori* principles which could only be discussed adequately in a separate study. But since in the chapter on the general problem no fewer than eight principles about goodness which could be proposed as likely *synthetic a priori* principles were held to be false it seems reasonable to believe that satisfactory principles will probably not be found. The question is noted here as a possible non-theist position which the study has not discussed. The study has dealt with problems about logical compatibility raised for theism by evil and claimed that none of them can be shown to be decisive.[1]

NOTES

[1] Similar views on certain points have been expressed independently in a recent article by Keith E. Yandell ('Ethics, Evils and Theism', *Sophia*, Vol. VIII, No. 2 (1969)). He refers to two chapters of a book by Alvin Plantinga, indicating that the arguments used resemble some of those proposed in this study (*God and Other Minds*, Ithaca, New York, Cornell University Press, 1967, Chs. 5 and 6).

The indefinite conclusions that have been reached are consistent with Judaism and Christianity. Far from containing solutions to all of the *intellectual* problems raised by evil, both Jewish and Christian revelations leave the problems shrouded in mystery. (See, e.g., Job, Chs. 38–42; Rom., Ch. 11, 33–5.)

Bibliography

Books

AQUINAS, ST THOMAS, *Summa Contra Gentiles (On the Truth of the Catholic Faith)*, New York, Doubleday & Co. Inc., 1955, Bk. 3, Pt. 1.
Summa Theologiae, new English translation, ed. Dominican Fathers, London, Eyre & Spottiswoode, 1967, Vol. 8.

AUGUSTINE, ST, *Augustine: Confessions and Enchiridion*, trans. Albert C. Outler, Philadelphia, Westminster Press, 1955.
The City of God, trans. Marcus Dods, George Wilson and J. J. Smith, New York, Random House, Inc., 1950.

BAYLE, P., *Bayle's Historical and Critical Dictionary—Selections*, ed. Richard Popkin, Indianapolis, Bobbs Merrill, 1965.

BRADLEY, F. H., *Appearance and Reality*, London, Oxford University Press, 1930.

CAMPBELL, C. A., *On Selfhood and Godhood*, London, Allen & Unwin Ltd., 1957.

COPLESTON, F. C., *Aquinas*, Harmondsworth, Penguin, 1955.

D'ARCY, M., *The Pain of this World and the Providence of God*, Milwaukee, Bruce Publishing Co., 1935.

DUCASSE, C. J., *A Philosophical Scrutiny of Religion*, New York, Ronald Press, 1953.

FARRER, A., *Love Almighty and Ills Unlimited*, London, Collins, Fontana Library, 1962.

FERRE, N., *Evil and the Christian Faith*, New York, Harper & Row, 1947.

FLEW, A., *God and Philosophy*, London, Hutchinson, 1966.

HAWKINS, D. J. B., *The Essentials of Theism*, London and New York, Sheed & Ward, 1949.

HICK, J., *Evil and the God of Love*, London, Macmillan, 1966.
Philosophy of Religion, ed. E. and M. Beardsley, Englewood Cliffs, N.J., Prentice-Hall, Inc., 1963.

HUME, D., *Dialogues Concerning Natural Religion*, ed. Henry D. Aiken, New York, Hafner Publishing Co., 14th printing, 1966.

JOURNET, C., *The Meaning of Evil*, London, Geoffrey Chapman, 1963.

JOYCE, G. H., *Principles of Natural Theology*, London, Longmans, Green, 3rd edn., 1957.

LEIBNIZ, G. W., *Theodicy, Essays on the Goodness of God, the Freedom of Man and the Origin of Evil*, trans. E. M. Huggard, London, Routledge & Kegan Paul, 1952.

LEWIS, C. S., *The Problem of Pain*, London, Collins, Fontana Books, 6th impression, 1965.

LONERGAN, B. J. F., *Insight*, London, Longmans, Green, 1957.

MADDEN, E. H. and HARE, P. H., *Evil and the Concept of God*, Springfield, Illinois, Charles C. Thomas, 1968.

MARITAIN, J., *St. Thomas and the Problem of Evil*, Milwaukee, Marquette University Press, 1942.
God and the Permission of Evil, trans. Joseph W. Evans, Milwaukee, Bruce Publishing Co., 1965.

McTAGGART, J. M. E., *Some Dogmas of Religion*, London, Edward Arnold, 1906.

MILL, J. S., 'Nature', *Nature and Utility of Religion*, ed. G. Nakhnikian, New York, Liberal Arts Press, 1958.
An Examination of Sir William Hamilton's Philosophy, London, Longmans, Green, 1865.

PETIT, F., *The Problem of Evil*, trans. Christopher Williams, New York, Hawthorn Books, 1959.

PHILLIPS, D. Z., *The Concept of Prayer*, London, Routledge & Kegan Paul, 1965; New York, Schocken Books, 1966.

PLANTINGA, A., *God and Other Minds*, Ithaca, New York, Cornell University Press, 1967.

PONTIFEX, M., *Providence and Freedom*, London, Burns & Oates, Faith and Fact Books, 1960, Vol. 22.

SERTILLANGES, A. D., *Le Problème du Mal*, Paris, Aubier, 1951, 2 vols.

SIWEK, P., *The Philosophy of Evil*, New York, Ronald Press, 1956.

TEILHARD DE CHARDIN, P., *The Phenomenon of Man*, London, Collins, 1959.
The Divine Milieu, New York, Harper & Row, 1960.

TSANOFF, R. A., *The Nature of Evil*, New York, Macmillan Co., 1931.

VIENJEAN, J., *Love, Suffering, Providence*, trans. Joan Marie Roth, Westminster, Maryland, Newman Press, 1966.

Articles

AIKEN, H. D., 'God and Evil: Some Relations between Faith and Morals', *Ethics*, Vol. LXVIII (1958).

BRADLEY, R. D., 'A Proof of Atheism', *Sophia*, Vol. VI, No. 1 (1967).

FARRELL, P. M., 'Evil and Omnipotence', *Mind*, Vol. LXVII (1958).

FLEW, A., 'Are Ninian Smart's Temptations Irresistible?', *Philosophy*, Vol. XXXVII (1962).

'Divine Omnipotence and Human Freedom', *New Essays in Philosophical Theology*, ed. A. Flew and A. MacIntyre, New York, Macmillan Co., 1955.

'Theology and Falsification', *op. cit.*

GRAVE, S. A., 'On Evil and Omnipotence', *Mind*, Vol. LXV (1956).

MACKIE, J. L., 'Evil and Omnipotence', *Mind*, Vol. LXX (1961). This article is reprinted in *God and Evil*, ed. Nelson Pike, Englewood Cliffs, New Jersey, Prentice-Hall, Inc., 1964.

'Evil and Omnipotence', *Mind*, Vol. LXIV (1955).

'Theism and Utopia', *Philosophy*, Vol. XXXVII (1962).

'Omnipotence', *Sophia*, Vol. I, No. 2 (1962).

MAYO, B., 'Mr Keene on Omnipotence', *Mind*, Vol. LXX (1961).

McCLOSKEY, H. J., 'God and Evil', *Philosophical Quarterly*, Vol. X (1960). Reprinted in *God and Evil*.

'The Problem of Evil', *Journal of Bible and Religion*, Vol. XXX (1962).

PIKE, N., 'Hume on Evil', *Philosophical Review*, Vol. LXXII (1963). Reprinted in *God and Evil*.

PLANTINGA, A., 'The Free Will Defence', *Philosophy in America*, ed. Max Black, London, Allen & Unwin Ltd., 1965.

SMART, N., 'Omnipotence, Evil and Supermen', *Philosophy*, Vol. XXXVI (1961). Reprinted in *God and Evil*.

WATKIN, E. I., 'The Problem of Evil', *God and the Supernatural*, ed. Father Cuthbert, OFM Cap., London and New York, Sheed & Ward, abridged edn., 1936.

WISDOM, J., 'God and Evil', *Mind*, Vol. XLIV (1935).

YANDELL, K., 'Ethics, Evils and Theism', *Sophia*, Vol. VIII, No. 2 (1969).

ZIMMERMAN, M., 'A Note on the Problem of Evil', *Mind*, Vol. LXX (1961).

Index

omnipotence—*cont.*
  exercise of, 20 n.9
  implications of, 20 n.9
  paradoxes of, 14–15
omniscience, 16, 74–5

pain, *see* suffering
Phillips, D. Z., 12 n.16, 20 n.9
physical evil, 4, 18, 24–5, 26–7, 31,
  34–7, 45–50 *passim*
Pike, Nelson, 11 n.1
Plantinga, Alvin, 79 n.1
power, finite, ix–x, 20 n.1
  omnipotent, ix, 13–16
principles, need of, 22, 33
  about goodness, 34, 36–7, 41 n.30,
    78
  about power, 34, 41 n.16
  discussed, 34–8 *passim*, 41 n.30,
    46, 47–8
  synthetic a priori, xiii n.2, 4 n.17,
    78–9
privation theory, 19
'problem of evil', 1–2, 9–11
problems of evil, 1–11 *passim*
  kinds of, 1–9
  relation between, 5–9, 43, 50 n.2,
    76 n.7
  as unavoidable, xi–xii, xiii n.13
psychological evil, 4, 18, 24–5, 26–7,
  29, 31, 34–7, 45–50 *passim*

Rhees, Rush, 20 n.9

Romans, Epistle to the, 79 n.1

Sertillanges, A. D., 21 n.13, 76 n.4
Smart, Ninian, 77 nn.25, 33
Specific abstract problems, nature of,
  6–7, 42, 50 n.2
  about degrees and multiplicity,
    46–50
  discussed, 43–50
  about kinds, 45–6
specific concrete problems, *see* concrete problems
Steen, John W., 11 n.3
Stevenson, C. L., xii n.6
suffering, animal, 18, 43–5 *passim*,
  68
  human, 18, 41 n.15, 44, 63–5
    passim, 65–8 *passim*, 70–1
  of innocent, 51 n.9, 66, 67–8
  nature of, 19
synthetic a priori principles, *see* principles

traditional problem, *see* general
  problem

Weil, Simone, 20 n.9
Whitehead, A. N., 20 n.1
Wisdom, John, 32, 52 n.12
world, uncreated but dependent,
  xiii n.3

Yandell, Keith, 79 n.1